To Anne,

with best wishes,

Victor

Fleeing the Nazis, Surviving the Gulag, and Arriving in the Free World

Fleeing the Nazis, Surviving the Gulag, and Arriving in the Free World

My Life and Times

Victor Zarnowitz

PRAEGER

Westport, Connecticut
London

Library of Congress Cataloging-in-Publication Data

Zarnowitz, Victor, 1919–
    From wartime Auschwitz and the Gulag to the free world : my life and times / Victor Zarnowitz.
       p.   cm.
    Includes bibliographical references and index.
    ISBN 978–0–313–35778–7 (alk. paper)
    1. Zarnowitz, Victor, 1919–   2. Economists—United States—Biography.
3. Holocaust survivors—United States—Biography.   I. Title.
    HB119.Z37A3   2008
    330.092—dc22   2008016489
    [B]

British Library Cataloguing in Publication Data is available.

Library of Congress Catalog Card Number: 2008016489
ISBN: 978–0–313–35778–7

First published in 2008

Praeger Publishers, 88 Post Road West, Westport, CT 06881
An imprint of Greenwood Publishing Group, Inc.
www.praeger.com

Printed in the United States of America

∞™

The paper used in this book complies with the Permanent Paper Standard issued by the National Information Standards Organization (Z39.48–1984).

10 9 8 7 6 5 4 3 2 1

Contents

Foreword

The common path that Victor Zarnowitz and the Conference Board have followed for over a decade began in 1996. In that year, the Conference Board assumed responsibility from the U.S. Department of Commerce for publishing the Leading Economic Indicators and became stewards of the larger business cycle indicators program. Victor is a true intellectual pioneer in this important field of economic research and became a member of the Conference Board's Business Cycle Indicators Advisory Panel in 1996.

In 1999, Victor accepted our invitation to serve in a permanent role as Senior Fellow and Economic Counselor to the Conference Board, becoming our mentor and friend, as well as our colleague. During the past decade he has helped to construct and launch Leading Economic Indexes for eight countries in addition to the United States, and has also played a critical role in developing the Conference Board's economic research program to the level of globally recognized excellence it enjoys today.

As you read this gripping story, you will get to know a man of integrity, drive, and a strong spirit. When Poland was invaded by the Germans, Victor left what had been his home for most of his formative years, the town of Oświęcim that later became, in German, Auschwitz. The very name conjures up suffering, death, and genocide on an unprecedented scale. But for Victor, in the years 1929 to 1939, it was a simple town full of school, concerts, sports, and friends—with few hints of the drastic turn of events that lay ahead.

On September 2, 1939, Victor and his brother, Tadek, began a long journey east into the unknown, to Brzezany beyond Lwow, newly occupied by the Soviets, and ultimately to prison and work camp. Victor tells this as a simple story, and yet his history charts among the saddest and the most hopeful moments in human history.

As we benefit from the security and peace in the modern world, it is easy to forget the pain and crisis, the uncertainty, the volatility, and the random events that marked almost every aspect of political and economic life for many in much of the pre-World War II period. The deep questions and motivations that drive our own lives—let alone the lives of others—are never crystal clear. And yet, as we, his colleagues and friends, reflect on this extraordinary man and his personal history, the question, "Can we not do better?" resonates loudly from his life and professional accomplishment.

Victor is a man who has dedicated his life to analysis, to establishing an empirical framework, a body of knowledge, and a climate of debate that demonstrates firmly and factually that we can do better. We can anticipate change—whether personal, political, or economic—and take constructive action to shape our present as well as our future. We are all fortunate that Victor survived his own personal long march to come the great distance to our world, and contribute in such a special way to both the field of economics and America's intellectual life.

Gail D. Fosler,
President, The Conference Board
June 2008

Introduction

This book reveals to readers the remarkable history and development of one of the world's most productive economic scientists, Victor Zarnowitz. In spite of incredible hardships endured during the dark Nazi period of the twentieth century, he emerged to become a remarkably successful student with a Ph.D. degree in economics, *summa cum laude*, from the University of Heidelberg in 1951. Then he went on to experience a great career in lecturing, research, and consulting at leading universities in the United States. He is currently Professor Emeritus of Economics and Finance, Graduate School of Business, University of Chicago, a Research Associate at the National Bureau of Economic Research, and Economic Advisor at The Conference Board. He has received many honors including being elected Fellow of the American Statistical Association, Fellow of the National Association of Business Economists, and Honorary Fellow of the International Institute of Forecasters. Also, he received the William F. Butler Award from the New York Association for Economists. And his many important books and research papers have earned him worldwide recognition as a leading researcher in the fields of business cycles, forecasting, forecast evaluation, and macroeconomics as noted by many who attended a 2003 European research conference in his honor.

As explained in this book, Victor's scientific research is characterized not by "measurement without theory" nor by "theory without measurement" but by a wholesome emphasis on "theory with measurement." Indeed, in his teaching and research, he has devoted much work and study to understand old and new theories so as to be able to test them in a meaningful manner. And in addition to this valuable work, he has always emphasized the importance of having good data to implement and/or test theories. His emphasis on "measurement with theory" was something that appealed to many others and me and is reflected in almost all of his published books and papers. And to make his research even more attractive to many, Victor placed a strong emphasis on measuring the forecasting or predictive performance of alternative models and theories. Indeed, he is often given credit for developing basic scientific procedures and norms for the evaluation of forecasts provided by different models and forecasters using a variety of methods and models. He is indeed a pioneer in this and many other areas of business cycle and forecasting research for which we are all very grateful.

On a more personal level, reading this book revealed to me Victor's great success in creating a wonderful family, an outstanding career, and a very constructive and friendly personality over the years since coming to the United States. He overcame the hatred and bitterness associated with his dismal past. And indeed, his heartwarming and glowing remarks about the freedom, opportunities, legal protections, etc. of the United States confirmed the experiences of many others with immigrant pasts that involved much suffering who also appreciated very much their experiences in the United States. It is indeed fortunate that Victor did not give up but rather worked hard to achieve his dreams, for which we are all very grateful.

Arnold Zellner
University of Chicago
June 2008

Prologue: A Vanished World

It is Sunday, September 13, 2004, and I am on a slow Polish train from Kraków to Oświęcim, the small town where I grew up. When I was a teenager, no one outside the district had ever heard of it, but it had long since become the most notorious town on earth. The German name for Oświęcim is Auschwitz.

We stop at eleven small stations, and the name of each is familiar. This is the fourth time since World War II that I have traveled this route. But, in earlier days I rode this train daily. In 1938 and 1939 I had commuted to law school in Kraków. I can still remember those years, when the pall of impending crisis began to engulf us.

People from all over come to see the SS extermination camps. So do I, but with an additional and more personal purpose, namely to see the house where I grew up. This dear place of my childhood and youth is close to the Auschwitz railroad station, and only several minutes' walk from the camp the Nazis later built at the end of the line in nearby Birkenau.

There is a sprawling new gas station next door, but the house, which my mother and grandmother had built for us, is still standing in "Narrow" Street. This is not a surprise. When you go back to Poland, you don't find familiar faces, old friends, or families. But you find the same houses, which remain because no one is rich enough to destroy them.

My brother, mother, grandmother, and I had left on September 2, 1939, the second day of the war. I next saw the house in late 1946. Then, one of the walls had been cracked by a Russian shell. A Polish couple had moved in. They were suspicious of me, wondering if I wanted to claim it back. But I had no desire to stay in Poland. All I wanted then was to flee to America with my new family. I agreed to sell the house to them for a few dollars. I felt lucky to get that much.

I ring the doorbell and am greeted by new owners, a young Polish couple. They know nothing about the house's history, except that it may have been built long ago by a Jewish family. They do not invite me in, but are kind and we have a good conversation in the garden. The property seems to be reasonably well maintained. They are curious to know more details about the house's history, and I tell them. It is a familiar story, one that could also be told about hundreds of thousands of other houses all around Poland.

I spend the rest of the day walking around the town of Oświęcim itself, which lies at some distance across the river Soła. It is at once different and the same as I remember it. The old castle on the hill retains its near-medieval appearance. The marketplace, otherwise well preserved, is marred by a large and hideous department store at its very center. I am told that people complain about this and that the eyesore may be removed. The river is now bordered by a good-looking park but I yearn for the sandy and stony beaches of my memory.

I eat at a small restaurant and talk to people, while trying to spot older types who might remember my town of long ago. Some try to be helpful, but everyone is a stranger to the old times and place, so we have trouble sharing common interests and language. The most common talk is about high prices, low wages, and lack of jobs. Life is so much better abroad, particularly in America, and it is the politicians' fault. Actually, as an economist fresh back from international business meetings, I know that the current conditions in Poland are relatively good. But locally some big factories have closed and jobs are hard to find. A big new hotel recently built near the station stands largely vacant. I am told lots of tourists come to see the camp but stay only a few hours and then return to Kraków the same day.

A trip to an annihilation camp like Birkenau can and probably should produce a painful horror shock followed by a deep and cathartic sorrow. It is not an experience to be readily repeated, least of all for someone who lived in Oświęcim before, in normal times. A visit to the same town after the Holocaust is likewise apt to be depressing and frustrating. Why then do I feel drawn to this place time and again, even sixty-five years after I fled it?

I do not hope to find answers to the great questions of the age, such as progress and moral values ("How can German culture be reconciled with the Holocaust?") or theodicy ("How can an all-merciful and almighty God have let the Holocaust happen?"). Rather, my motivation is the search for the continuity and meaning of my own life. This effort requires a mental reconstruction of my past, and physical contacts with places in which I have lived may help. My earlier visits to Oświęcim, Kraków, and Łańcut, the town of my birth, lent support to this belief, although I probably would cling to it as a matter of faith anyway.

My return in 1946, after wartime exile in the Soviet Union, led to such a sudden revelation of the horrors of the Holocaust that I could not summon the courage to walk from my family house to the Birkenau camp. People who lived here talked about the years of nightmare in the simplest and starkest terms: the incessant smoke from the chimneys, the stench of human flesh burning, all that which had struck them most immediately. Moreover, there was not a soul among these people that I could recall knowing in the ten years I had lived here before the war.

It was only much later, in 1974, that I was able for the first time to see the Birkenau camp, that place of quick execution for most, and of slow torture for many. About a million Jews died in the Auschwitz camps, and half a million other inmates, including a great many Soviet prisoners of war. I didn't really need to see any of this museum of human evil. The very thought that it had happened (and in "my" Oświęcim, too!) is often enough to bring tears to my eyes.

My third trip to Oświęcim was in the fall of 2001, when I was better prepared for the inevitable shock of once again facing the famous gate with the mock inscription "Work Makes Free." This time I was able to say a *Kaddish* at the memorial near the crematorium. It was good to be there and offer the prayer for the dead, even in a place where it is most difficult to sustain belief. It was impossible not to be aware that the whole world of my youth is gone.

I feel somehow driven or impelled to go back to Poland, and it's a very sad journey each time. I know what I'm going to experience. Nothing is surprising about it anymore. There's no one there.

If you do not attend to your own life, who will? Can you be of use to anyone if you are of no use to yourself? Plato famously said, "The life which is unexamined is not worth living." The consciousness of life's meaning enhances its quality. But when and how is life to be "examined" so that it is rendered valuable? Surely, self-examination, which must aim at self-knowledge and self-improvement, is an act of will that takes time and effort. A man is a thinking and remembering being, but life precedes thought and deserves attention as a whole, not preconditioned on the degree to which it turned out to be lucky, successful, valuable, or fulfilled.

Memory has a large role in contemplating life. Early memories are important; unfortunately, they tend to be selective and fade. So, a memoir—an attempt to revive memory and reexamine life—has a deep personal function. Memoirs, and written histories, have an important, more general service to perform as well. They preserve and transmit knowledge to successive generations.

Psychologists know that when the present is cheerful, then often the recollected past is too, and when the present looks gloomy, so does the past. But it is probably also true that many are biased—in one or the other direction—independently of the mood of the day. Some tend to suppress the unhappy and prettify the happy memories; for others, the negatives overwhelm the positives. My own early life had much of the tragic in it, so I have to guard mostly against the pessimistic bias.

Where a disaster such as virulent persecution decimates the families of a particular nation, the need to remember and share becomes more acute. The holocaust of 1939–1945 remains the most horrifying event of this type in recent history, and even in the long and incredibly cruel history of the Jews in exile. No wonder, then, that stories of personal and family tragedies during the Holocaust continue to dominate contemporary memoirs in literature and the arts.

My own experience of wartime survival unfolded in the camps and villages of the former Soviet Union, but I lost most of my family to the Nazis. My memoir follows the tracks of my extended family, on my father and mother's sides, through the prewar, World War II, and postwar periods. Fighting against the difficulty to remember, I made a strong effort to collect all the information I could about those who perished and those who have survived.

This is our story.

And Music Was in the Air

1 ■ ■ ■ I was born on November 3, 1919. I do not know whether my birth was in a hospital or at home, and for many years now there has been no one left to tell me. By doctor or midwife, the event sparked little interest around the small town of Łańcut* in southeastern Poland. My first cries may have been lost in the clatter of carpenters at work. Almost exactly one year had passed since the end of World War I.

Poland remained in conflict with the Soviets, and a final peace would not be reached for two more years, but Łańcut, at least, was no longer near the front lines. Here, as in most of Europe, the inhabitants were vigorously rebuilding. Besides sawing and hammering, there was the scramble of commerce renewed, and the chatter of political debate. After a century and a half of servitude under powerful neighbors who partitioned their country, the Polish people were finally a sovereign nation once more.

My father, Leopold, was in his thirties. He and his wife had just staggered through the trauma of World War I. In 1913, when my brother had been born, my father was teaching in Brzeżany, which like all southern Poland was then part of Austria–Hungary. He had not been a combatant in the fighting. As a teacher he was an employee of the government, and perhaps that exempted him from service. Nevertheless, the war severed him from the life he had known.

---

*Pronounced Wan'tsut.

Only six years separated my brother's birth from mine, but by 1919 the Austro-Hungarian Empire no longer existed. My father remained a state employee, but the state was now Poland, and he had been transferred to Łańcut. Whatever he had faced during the interval—and, as usual, Poland had suffered cruelly in the war—by the time of my birth, those difficulties were the past. It was November 1919, and my parents were burning wood against the severe winter, but for the first time in five years, they might securely predict a cheerful spring.

Our family was close and affectionate. Each of us was known by several names. My father, a philologist with a hatful of languages at his command, was Leopold in Polish, Loeb in Yiddish, and Arie in Hebrew. My mother was Bertha, otherwise Miriam, but known to all by the diminutive, Mitzi. Teodor, or Theodore, my brother, was affectionately called Tadek, or Tadzio. My Hebrew name is Ze'ev, my Jewish name is Wolf, but I was always known as Victor, or endearingly as Wicek. But, I had another nickname, which I earned the hard way. As a toddler, I had heedlessly run too close to a chained dog, which had lunged, snapped, and bitten me above the right eye. Doctors feared for my vision, but in the end the only results were a small scar and an early nickname, *Wscieklizna*, the "Wild One."

I remember Łańcut as romantically beautiful. The time I spent there, as a boy, was a magical period. Looking back at those years, I see a family young, happy, and together. This was the one and only phase of my life full of harmony and happiness, free of all sense of loss, sin, and evil. My parents and brother had moved there shortly before I was born. My father taught German, Latin, and Greek to students at the local gymnasium, which was more or less equivalent to an American high school.

At the center of the community was Łańcut Palace, home to Count Alfred Potocki, playboy and diplomat, scion of one of Poland's richest families, blood relation to every royal house in Europe. None of the Count's exalted guests, neither Franz Ferdinand of Austria nor the Duke of Kent, could boast a finer mansion than his 200-room castle. Approaching it in their host's coach and six, the visitors passed the narrow, unpaved streets in town, the houses pressing in on either side. Opening the wide market square, the servant outriders sounded a horn as long as the carriage itself. Vendors and bargain-hunters quit haggling and stepped aside to make a lane.

In the 1600s, the castle had been a crucial point in Poland's southern defenses, but the bastions and ramparts had long since been replaced by a formal English park. Inside, armories and barracks had become ballrooms and salons. Guests could play polo, ride to hounds on the Count's 40,000 acres, or visit his famous Arabians in their huge yellow stables. And if they did, they might have noticed a small boy peering through the fence. The stables were right across Sienna Street from our modest home and I often watched the magnificent creatures, and their at times even more impressive riders.

Seeing them as a child, I did not think in terms of rich or poor. The Potocki family lived inside their palace, mysterious and rarely seen. They were a different species. Their stables were far larger than the house we shared with two other families. Our home was built from wood and occupied a single, low-slung story. We were on the right side, and on the left was a Polish lawyer with his wife and two sons. A widow, Pani Dzierżyńska, resided in the middle of the house. In a fearful climate where the new Soviet Union was hardly discussed, I had only heard rumors that she was related to Feliks Dzierżyński, the first head of the Soviet secret police. Behind the house, in spring and summer, the garden was filled with bushes—bluish, violet, reddish, and whitish lilacs of brilliant color and fragrance.

Inside, my father's library was my favorite room. I was drawn to it even as a small child. I could read before I started school at the age of six, and the great leather books, stacked behind glass panes, offered hours and hours of interest. I would have to grow into the Goethe and Schiller, the epics from Greece and Rome, and the English and French works in translation. But I immediately took to the illustrated fables of the Brothers Grimm, Andersen, the *Thousand and One Nights*, the adventures of *Robinson Crusoe*, and the *Three Musketeers*. I recall the photographs in "Die Völker des Erde" and "Die Tiere des Erde," two massive German volumes that divided all life into the peoples and animals of the Earth.

One book, though small, was treated with more reverence than the rest. It was a little leather manuscript, the *Megillat Ester*, or Book of Esther, that had been beautifully written by my father's father, a Hebrew scribe. He had died before I was born and this single book was the only artifact we had from him. A scribe was of necessity a religious man, yet my grandfather had possessed the magnanimity to allow his sons to grow up in the modern fashion. Or, perhaps they were strong willed and gave him no choice. My father, the middle child, was born in a small town in the 1880s, but it was a liberal era, and he spent many of his young adult years in Vienna, at a time when Jews enjoyed a high degree of acceptance there.

Emperor Franz Joseph was a progressive monarch, considered to be "good for the Jews." Feeling comfortable enough to assimilate, my father's next of kin fled the religious life for the professions. The eldest brother had gone into business as a furrier in the Leopoldstadt, Vienna's Jewish neighborhood. With the money from his shop he had put both of his siblings through college. Father studied languages, and my youngest uncle became a lawyer. They were the first in my family to get university educations. Yet, no matter how comfortable Vienna might have seemed, a Jewish man was never really allowed to forget who he was. During these same years, while my father was earning his degree, a young artist named Adolf Hitler lived in the city; he had just been rejected from the art academy and his bitterness was growing.

The Jews in Łańcut, like those across Europe, had persevered through periods of tolerance and near-acceptance that alternated with ages of persecution. The first Jewish residents had arrived in our town by 1563. In the 1700s, local Catholics forced all Jews to hide in their homes with the doors locked and the windows shut during church processions. In the 1800s, on the other hand, the townspeople celebrated the construction of the Great Synagogue, a beautiful temple in Baroque style.[1] In good and bad years, the Jews held on. By the time I was born, we numbered nearly half the town's population. There were 3,500 Jews in Łańcut, and many, many different ways of being Jewish.

The Hassidim and Orthodox rabbis retained much of their ancient influence, yet the younger generation was widely considered to be *maskilim*, a Hebrew word meaning enlightened, modern, secular. Zionism was no longer a new movement. A few years before I was born it had been a forbidden secret society; by the 1920s it was thriving and respectable. In our small town, there were at least a dozen different Zionist groups—ranging from socialist to extremely religious—that were always in conflict with non-Zionists and each other.

Our family was very secular. Except on High Holidays, and some Sabbaths, we rarely appeared at the synagogue. We spoke Polish, not Yiddish, at home. My father was a modern man. He wore fashionable suits, which looked as if he ordered them from Vienna. He thought of himself as a citizen of Poland, and indeed he had spent much of his life trying to assimilate. Yet, he had learned the lesson that Europe, even in an age of acceptance, had taught him that no matter how you see yourself, others would always see you as a Jew.

He had been the scholar in his family, and it was likely that I would be the scholar in ours. He encouraged me to read, and one day he entered the library while I was there. Perhaps I was leafing through "The People of the Earth," and had to quickly flip the page away from photos of bare-breasted savage women when I heard his footsteps. Retrieving the *Megillat Ester* that his father had written from its place of honor, he told me of the accomplishments of the Jews. It was our ancestors who had given the world the Bible, he told me, and nothing could ever change that. Speaking in a serious voice, in the kind of tone intended to imprint itself on a young boy's memory, he said, "We are the people of the book."

■ ■ ■

I was one of those students—a small minority in any place or time—who truly enjoyed going to school. When, a little after dawn, mother crept in to rouse us, I was usually already awake. Father was at the breakfast table reading the day's issue of *Czas*, a rather conservative Polish newspaper published in Kraków. Tadek and I ate quickly and then took the short walk to elementary school, just a few blocks away. Classes began at 8:00 A.M. Miss Rutkowska, my teacher the entire time I spent in Łańcut, taught every subject, including behavior and comportment. I was an "A" student in nearly all the disciplines; the best in the class in languages, history, and geography, near the top in science and mathematics. Proving that I had outgrown my reputation as a "wild one," I even got excellent marks in behavior and comportment.

A wooden crucifix was nailed to the wall in each classroom of the public school. In the mornings, the Catholics all prayed together, chanting the *Pater Noster* in unison, while we Jewish students (roughly one-third of the class) stood in silence.[2] During religion lessons, the Jews stood on the side of the room. Hebrew was not offered as a language of study, and I struggled through my lessons in the afternoons with a private tutor. After that, if I didn't also have piano lessons, and had finished my schoolwork, I could play *palant*, a game like baseball, with the other kids in the neighborhood.

More often, though, Tadek and I would stay in our room and act out little performances. We would assume the roles of characters we'd been studying in school or reading about at home. One evening, Tadek might play Achilles while I became Hector (since he was older and bigger, he was frequently the winner). On another he became Edmond Dantes, the future Count of Monte Cristo, and I, the younger, might play the old Abbe Faria, who directed Dantes to the hidden treasure and helped him escape to claim it. These plays, perhaps best described as a childish *commedia dell'arte*, were for our own enjoyment only. Had any audience been present, even our parents, we would have been far too self-conscious to perform.

Scrubbed and ravenous, we'd gather in the kitchen for dinner. Market Day, when farmers from the outlying villages drove their carts into the Square, was Thursday, but many of the vegetables on the table came from our own garden. While not strictly kosher, we did not eat pork. The cuisine was a mix of German, Austrian, Hungarian, Czech, Polish, and Jewish. My favorite dishes were pierogi, or rice and cherries drenched in *smetana* cream. After dinner, we turned on the radio. On Friday evenings, once the sun went down, the Jewish part of Łańcut became quiet and still — Shabbas had begun. On Saturdays, our shops were closed and the Catholics' were open. On Sundays, it was reversed. On either day, half the community was at prayer.

The Polish calendar was riddled with Saint's Days and religious observances. There was also November 11, Armistice Day, commemorating the recent peace. Two festivals, celebrated just a few days apart, stood out. On May 1, the laborers held their May Day, marching with banners and ostentatiously skipping work. But that was an unofficial event. Two days later, May 3, was Constitution Day, Poland's equivalent to July 4.

On May 3, 1791, the Polish Parliament had ratified a liberal, modern constitution.[3] Founded on the same egalitarian principles that had sparked the American and French revolutions, the document was threatening to the established monarchies of Central and Eastern Europe. Soon, Prussia, Russia, and Austria invaded and divided Poland. For the next 125 years, there had been no independent Polish nation in Europe. During that long period of servitude, the May 3rd Constitution had remained as a beacon and rallying cry for those who dreamed of a return to sovereignty.

To achieve the goal, though, would take more than dreams. It would take three insurrections and finally a world war.

The people of Poland long considered it a tragic fact of geography to be situated between the Germans and Russians. For centuries, the armies of both these nations had marched and countermarched across the country. During World War I, the situation was more intolerable than ever, and no area suffered worse than Galicia, the district where Łańcut was located. "Like hosts of termites the contending armies moved backward and forward," Count Potocki recalled, "stripping the land bare and reducing farms and villages to rubble and shattered timber."[4] The Count himself had little to fear. After all, Kaiser Wilhelm II was his godfather, and the commanders of both armies gave orders to leave his estates untouched. Still, the troubles of war touched even Łańcut Castle, where "various pieces of china and the like were missing." Potocki's second-story rooms were "dirty beyond description," and someone had stolen his shoes.

In the surrounding countryside, the peasants had real worries. They were ordered to burn their crops and food stores. After just the first year of the war, 70 percent of Galicia had been ruined, and looked as if it "had been destroyed by some terrific earthquake." Relief workers reported that "dogs are running wild with hunger . . . and flocks of crows and ravens in search of food are digging out with their beaks the shallow graves of Russian and Teutonic soldiers."[5] The Czar's soldiers were just a few miles distant when Potocki drove away in his Mercedes, bearing only "a few guns, furs and a change of clothing."[6] The roads had been damaged by shells, and were clogged—not for the last time—by Jewish refugees fleeing Łańcut and the approaching enemy.

By 1918, with the United States in the war, the Czar overthrown, and Germany's defeat looking likely, Poland's time had come at last. President Woodrow Wilson arrived at Versailles to negotiate the peace. With him he brought Fourteen Points, idealistic demands to end the imperial system and divide the nations of Europe into autonomous states. Point XIII required that, "an independent Polish state should be erected which should include the territories inhabited by indisputably Polish populations." Few of the Fourteen Points survived in their original form, but both France and England believed a strong Poland could serve as a buffer between Germany and Russia, so in May 1921, the new constitution was ratified.

An exultant document, its first sentence was roughly 150 words long. "In the name of Almighty God!," it began:

We, the Polish Nation, thankful to Providence for freeing us from a servitude of a century and a half... taking up the glorious tradition of the memorable Constitution of the Third of May... having in mind the... independent mother country, and desiring to establish her... on the eternal principles of right and liberty... and of securing equality to all citizens of the Republic... and the special protection of the state to labor... do enact and establish... this constitutional law.

For us, this beginning was nothing but a poetic flourish. Article 95 was our relevant passage, and it came pages and pages later. "The Republic of Poland," it read, "guarantees on its territory, to all, without distinction of extraction, nationality, language, race, or religion, full protection of life, liberty, and property." For the Jews in Łańcut, this was the real test of the constitution's value. Half of the town's population was Jewish, and in the entire nation Jews accounted for roughly 10 percent. For better or worse, Poland was a very, very Catholic country. Karol Wojtyla, born just six months later than I, less than one hundred miles from Łańcut, would, as Pope John Paul II, one day apologize for centuries of anti-Semitism. In the meantime, a lot of Poles simply thought their country housed too many Jews.

In Łańcut, in the 1920s, I had little sense of this. A Jew would have to be stupid to be completely unaware of these feelings. I was not stupid, but I was protected. There was anti-Semitism, I knew that, but perhaps I believed it didn't apply to me. I didn't feel threatened by it. The Republic was new and glorious, my teacher and my father told me so. Our neighbors, Polish boys about my age, visited with us on Hanukkah. We went to their apartment and marveled at their beautiful Christmas tree. On Constitution Day each year, we went to the town center—sometimes to 3rd of May Street itself—and cheered and cheered at the banners, the music, and the glorious, indomitable horsemen of the Polish cavalry.

■ ■ ■

Music was in the air. Fryderyk Chopin, born near Warsaw in the previous century, was a native son, and his presence was ubiquitous. Almost every town, including our own, had a Chopin Street. Many homes had a piano,

Leopold Zarnowitz, Victor's father.

and most families seemed to boast of one member who could really play well. Father was a music lover, so several afternoons each week, my brother and I came under the patient tutelage of a local piano instructor. Tadek showed potential, but I was clearly destined to be in the audience and not the orchestra. At night, the radio carried performances by Caruso, and our family sat together and listened to his amazing voice.

My favorite picture of my father shows a handsome man with black hair combed back.He is clean-shaven, as usual, except for a thin mustache. He wears a well-fitting dark overcoat, carries a walking stick, and an English bowler hat—the personification of British elegance, by way of Vienna. He never complained of his surroundings. On the contrary, he would go into raptures while telling Tadek and me of the beauty of our garden, the synagogue, the count's palace, and even the stars at night. But he was a man of culture and Łańcut was a provincial backwater. Reflecting on his life, I try to determine whether or not he was happy. Perhaps he felt stifled—not to say disappointed—by his standing as a high-school language teacher in an unimportant town. He certainly stood out, his style was *au courant*, his conversation always well-informed on the latest topics. He smoked cigarettes one after another. He prided himself on cosmopolitan tastes, traveled to the cities as often as he could, and always took pains to expose us to literature, music, and art.

One morning, he came to the bedroom before dawn. Though I had been anticipating this day for weeks, this was one of those rare occasions when someone had to wake me. We left the house in darkness and walked through the empty streets toward the railroad station, an hour's journey by foot. The sun rose as we left the town behind us. The wooden houses in the outlying village could have sprung from centuries earlier, but the depot was a brand new replacement for one destroyed in the war.

We took second-class tickets and settled in our pleasant, upholstered seats. After watering, the locomotive belched once or twice, the cars lurched, and Łańcut disappeared behind us. The stations filed by— Rzeszów, Dębica, Tarnów, and Bochnia—and then, after several hours, we steamed through the outlying suburbs, and into Kraków itself. I had traveled to cities before. Katowice, a smoky industrial center in Silesia, had seemed larger, but no place I had seen could compare with the ancient beauty of Kraków, Poland's spiritual capital.

Father conducted his business during the day. In the evening, I followed him through the busy streets to the Juliusz Słowacki Theater, an imposing Gothic copy of the grand Paris Opera. We took our seats. The musicians tuned their strings. The audience—fashionable and elegant—gossiped around us. Father pointed out the finer points of the theater's architecture. The lights dimmed. The buzzing stopped. The orchestra struck three severe and insolent chords, and the curtains parted to reveal the church of *Sant'Andrea della Valle*. Puccini's *Tosca* had begun.

The playbill gave a brief plot summary in Polish, but I hardly needed it, let alone an understanding of Italian, to sense the tragedy of the story, or quail at the shocking horror of Tosca's fall. Afterward, I still made father answer question after question. We sang arias together on the train ride and later performed them for relatives. The train, Kraków, the opera house, the performance—we had both been transported far beyond the narrow confines of our daily lives.

■ ■ ■

My tenth birthday was a few weeks away. It was late summer of 1929. In the fields outside of town, Polish peasant boys of my age were busy at harvest, reaping a sorely needed bumper crop of rye and wheat.[7] School had begun again after the long holiday. Coming home one afternoon, I was surprised to find father there before me. The house was more crowded than usual, and tense. He had suffered some kind of episode during the day and had returned early. It was a heart attack, apparently a mild one, since by the morning he was already feeling much better. He was determined to return to work. The doctor assured him he could do so. Father, though a heavy smoker, was a healthy man in his mid-forties. He had probably just had a passing fit. Within a day or two, he was lecturing at the front of his classroom again.

I had a piano lesson after school. Halfway through, my mother came for me. We walked back to our house together, walked quickly, with, for me, a rising sense of panic. By the time I got home, he was dead. His second heart attack, less than a week after the first, but totally unforeseen, had been catastrophic. He was well dressed and elegant still. I looked at his body feeling emotions I can no longer summon or recall.

The gymnasium gave him a gorgeous funeral. His colleagues and students, dozens of them, followed the hearse out of town to the Jewish cemetery. We sat *shiva* at home. With the guests and our responsibilities as hosts, we were too busy to give ourselves up to grief. Then, after the last well-wisher had gone, mother took charge. She had all the furniture loaded onto a truck and driven to the station. My time in Łańcut was over. We were moving back in with mother's family in Oświęcim. Unknown and unimportant, except for its role as a hub for many crisscrossing railroad lines, the town had a different name in German: Auschwitz.

The Saddest Thing

2 ■ ■ ■ As a boy, I didn't comprehend that I was living through the greatest economic dislocation in history. My vision was far narrower. I knew times were hard for my family. My father had died in the fall of 1929, within weeks of the stock market crash in New York City. A depression had followed and before long spread to Europe. Poland, a newly created nation without established business relationships, still recovering from the World War I, and perpetually short of cash and credit, was especially vulnerable to the crisis.

My feelings were raw and deep, and I was intellectually keen for my age. Times were hard for my family after Father had died, and I was fully aware of this. But the very dominance of the private tragedy that befell us dimmed for me the impact of the public disaster that began unfolding all around.

A series of bad harvests of wheat, rye, and potatoes exacerbated the situation. The whole countryside was becoming destabilized; soon thousands would be fleeing their barren farms in favor of the cities. It felt like we were following the same path when, burdened with every stitch of clothing and stick of furniture we owned, we boarded the train for our new home. Oświęcim was a larger town than Łańcut. But Łańcut had been pastoral and romantic, while our destination was more modern, industrially and commercially.

I had made this same journey many times as a child, when we had often gone to stay with my mother's family during vacations. The train

Victor standing in front of his grandparent's former villa in Auschwitz in 2004.

ride was just a few hundred miles. The travel itself took five or six hours, but with coming and going, it was an all-day affair. When we arrived, the station had usually been as busy as a little city. Locomotives were being watered or repaired, porters loaded boxcars with bales and boxes. From Oświęcim merchants could send their goods anywhere: to Kraków in the east, Vienna in the south, or Katowice, Breslau, Berlin, and Hamburg to the west and north.[1]

The railroads had also provided a livelihood to my mother's parents, Emil and Olga Blumenfeld. Before World War I, they had owned and operated the restaurant inside the Auschwitz station. By the time I was born, they had sold out and gone into a comfortable retirement. But they hadn't gone far. Their elegant, gas-lighted villa was just a few steps from their former business, situated on Bahnhofstrasse (which, in English, means Railroad Station Street).

I had always looked forward to our visits. My grandmother no longer prepared meals for her customers, but she remained an excellent cook. I was a cute child, whom she loved to spoil, and the dinners she created, delicious and fun, were themselves worth the visit. I was close with my aunts, too. Fryda was eldest. Eda, with long, blond hair, and Paula, a pretty brunette, were playful and fun. The house had a good-sized garden and a nice orchard. There were cats and dogs, and a little aggressive she-goat without horns to play with. The king of the animals was a big (to me), but friendly, German shepherd, whom my father, ever the classicist, had named Dido. In the attic, I had found a forgotten treasure from the restaurant: an urn containing exotic coin from all over Europe.

In those happy days I had carried a valise filled with just enough clothes and books to last for a few weeks' stay. This time we were here for good. Perhaps, the train station was quieter when we arrived, showing the effects of economic stagnation. I walked to the familiar villa, but without my old sense of anticipation. Father was dead. My grandfather had also died recently, so my mother and grandmother were both new widows. Moving in together was the obvious decision, and each, I'm sure, was grateful for the support. We stayed with my grandmother for a few months, while our savings went to build a place where we would all live together. Just off the main road between the station and the town, the new house was far smaller than grandmother's old villa, but it had electricity.

My mother had been a strong presence throughout my childhood. She may have deferred to my father in most things, but with me and my brother she was always the stricter of the two, making sure our school work got done, and keeping us away from trouble. As a single parent she became even more of a force in my life. Looking back, I can imagine the burden she felt, the added responsibilities and stress of raising two boys on her own. Yet, she faced the challenge with strength and composure. Through all that difficult period, when she must have been desperately heartbroken and afraid, she never once broke down in front of me. I don't remember ever having seen her in tears. Witnessing her determination, I could hardly have done less myself.

By the end of 1930, one-third of the nation's industrial workers had lost their jobs, while the agricultural economy—lifeblood to a great majority of the population—had completely gone to seed.[2] Half of the entire budget was spent on the military, and the country's deficit was growing.[3] Desperate for more revenue, parliament ended all traces of prohibition, which, as in America, had been in effect since 1919. In Poland, the state had a monopoly on the sale of vodka and other spirits, so a drunker population meant a richer government. The number of sanctioned saloons almost doubled. Liquor became available on trains and could be sold at any time except the church hours on Sundays. When those measures didn't solve the problem, government employees had their salaries cut by 15 percent, and desperate legislators began to eye pensions, too.[4]

Things didn't get quite that far, which was lucky for us, since my father's pension was our main source of income. Even with that money, we steadily exhausted all our savings, and sold off what remained of grandmother's estate. Mother went to work for her older sister, Fryda's handicrafts store in Katowice. She was overseeing a number of girls working at their homes in Brzezinka nearby who embroidered women's undergarments. Even I helped out with this, by stenciling monograms in ink that were then stitched over by the girls. It was a rather stimulating experience, to handle the dainty unmentionables under the playful eyes of all those seamstresses.

Our other major concession to economy was the renting of an attic room in our house to a boarder. We were again fortunate because our tenant turned out to be director of the local cinema and he allowed us to see the movies for free. We drooled over Marlene Dietrich as *The Blue Angel*, and mimicked the cool toughness of Jean Gabin in *Pepe le Moko*, but it was the Hollywood films—the studios were at their absolute zenith—that we enjoyed the most. Jimmy Cagney, William Powell, and Errol Flynn gave us a sense of American culture. Sometimes that image was distorted, like when we saw the first talkie, Al Jolson's *The Jazz Singer*, in English with Polish subtitles. For the most part, America seemed far away. In Poland we had troubles and aspirations enough to keep us busy.

We didn't exactly go wanting, but still our family had to stretch every zloty to the limit. To earn some extra money, I tutored younger students. Teaching came naturally to me, and I would have been even better if I could have just kept organized. But unfortunately, my forgetfulness sometimes got in the way. This was a problem in daily life, too. I was around twelve years old when my mother showed her trust by giving me an important sum of money. I don't remember if I was supposed to buy something, or just hold on to it, but I think the bills totaled about twenty zlotys—the equivalent of four American dollars. It was beautiful currency, big and ornate, with the words "Bank Polski" in art-deco letters at the top. I understood the responsibility of holding the bills, but somehow I let them fall from my pocket. I lost the money.

My mother and I were walking together along the main street near the station and the three large brick buildings housing the railroad workers' apartments. Maybe she asked for the cash and I couldn't find it, or perhaps I confessed that the zlotys were gone. When she learned about the loss, she smacked me across the face, hitting my forehead with her open palm. She had never hit me before, and it never happened again. Until that moment she had seemed so calm in her adversity, almost imperturbable. But her emotion at the loss of a paltry sum of money showed the seriousness of our situation. We walked home together in silence, she, still furious, and probably remorseful, I, filled with indignation, just able to hold back the tears.

I entered gymnasium my first year in Oświęcim. Study had always been a major focus of my life. I had been a precocious child. Father had recognized my curiosity and encouraged it because my family valued education beyond almost anything else. Though I was at a different school, I was now as old as father's students had been when he was a teacher, and I was more determined than ever to excel.

St. Jan Kostka Gymnasium was a large red-brick building within walking distance of home. Named after a Polish saint and operated by the state, it was both the principal educational and patriotic institution in town. Entering the lobby each morning, we students passed under the inscribed Latin motto, "Dulce et decorum est pro patria mori." A quote from Horace's *Odes*, it translated to mean, "It is sweet and honorable to die for one's country." Now it seems strangely dark and foreboding, out of place in a house of learning. But at the time I remember thinking it was beautiful.

Many people of my age were proud and hopeful that we would be the first generation in centuries to grow up free, but we knew we were surrounded by powerful enemies and by much economic distress. In the west, Germany's economy was suffering badly as well. In 1933 its troubles and unrest had helped Adolf Hitler advance to the chancellorship. In the east, the Soviets had always been a menace. In 1920, two years after the rest of Europe had found peace, Polish forces under Marshal Jozef Piłsudski had routed the Red Army near Warsaw in a battle we all referred to as "the Miracle on the Vistula."

Piłsudski was our national hero, and in 1926, he launched a coup and took power. Though he was swift to silence any opposition, his transgressions were minor compared to those of the other strong men of the period. He was a benign dictator, if there can be such a thing. The whole school—and nation—mourned his death in 1935, and I wept along with others when I heard the news.

The gymnasium focused on a humanistic curriculum, stressing languages and history, subjects in which I had always done well. I studied Latin for five years, and also German, which was easy, since I already knew it. Classes met six days a week, and because school was open on Saturdays—our sabbath—few religious Jewish students enrolled. I was good looking and popular, and also quite assimilated, acknowledged by my teachers and colleagues as one of the most promising pupils in school. I had no sense whatsoever of being ghettoized. And yet, looking back, I see that all of my professors were Catholic, and all my closest friends—Jacob "Kuba" Szancer, Mordechai "Motek" Szwechter, and Stefan Reich— were Jewish. This fact didn't strike me as unusual at the time, but it could hardly be irrelevant. Like me, they were all good students, too, which may have helped to bring us together. We would study on our own during the periods of the day when our Christian schoolmates were learning religion.

The Polish Republic preached tolerance and equality, but the Polish people had a long history of widespread anti-Semitism, which no constitution could eradicate. Since its founding, the state had wrestled with this tension. Pogroms were so frequent in the early years of the Republic that the allied powers forced the government to enact a Minorities Treaty to protect the property and safety of the Polish Jews.[5] The first president of the Republic, Gabriel Narutowicz, had been elected thanks to the support of centrists, peasants, and left-wingers, but the reactionary National Democrats labeled him the "President of the Jews," and he was assassinated five days after his inauguration.

In Oświęcim, as recently as 1900, the residents had not been so very far removed from a medieval state of anti-Semitism, as this contemporary report describes:

Our oppressors laid a false charge of blood-libel against the Jews in the wake of the disappearance of a Christian maiden before Passover and witnesses testified that the Jews had brought her to the Jewish cemetery for burial. All the efforts of the police had so far been in vain. Lo and behold, the maiden was found by the Prussian police in Jast on the Prusso-Silesian border, where she had gone after her lover, to the boundless joy of the Jews in Oświęcim.[6]

By the 1930s, the gentiles had evolved beyond declaring blood-libels, to rigging the local government. Although Jews accounted for far more than half the population, the town laws mandated that only half the council could be Jewish at any given time.[7] On the national level, the number of Jews in the parliament, or *Sejm*, had dropped from thirty-six to five. While forbidden to take their share of political power, Jews were required to carry an extra economic burden. Not only were Jews barred from government employment and many industries, they were also taxed at a higher rate than their gentile neighbors. Though making up only 10 percent of the population, Polish Jews supplied 20 percent of the national revenue.[8]

I had yet to have my first personal experience of anti-Semitism, though I could have hardly remained unaware of its existence. When President Mościcki visited the town on one of his tours of the nation, I accompanied my fellow citizens to the main road to watch his progress—the Polish people dearly loved a parade—and cheered with all the rest, just as I had in Łańcut on May 3, 1900. Poland was my country, I had no doubt of that.

■ ■ ■

The Soła and Vistula rivers meet near Oświęcim, and I spent many lazy afternoons with my friends swimming or relaxing on the banks. We discussed the latest news or commentaries in the *Forward*, a socialist daily paper, or *Our Survey*, a Jewish paper from Kraków. We might commiserate or quiz each other about our approaching *matura* exams, the all-important tests that would decide whether or not we were to go on to university. The situation in Palestine had never seemed more important. And, as the decade progressed, we all watched nervously as Germany rearmed and grew more militant.

But, few topics of conversation wiled away more hours, led to as much fevered speculation, or occupied a larger proportion of our waking thoughts, than the subject of Marta and Danka. Marta was the most popular girl in the school, Polish of course, and completely unattainable. Danka was on a smaller scale, but equally out of my league. I knew them, and chatted with them in school, but never could summon the courage to ask either out on a date. I did, however, spend more than a few evenings lingering under Danka's balcony, hoping to catch a glimpse of her through the glass.

I can't say my intentions toward Marta and Danka were wholly innocent, but they would probably seem so by today's standards. Our passions were the same, but our behavior was very different. Sex during the gymnasium years was almost totally unknown, the students themselves would have considered it improper. And, despite our contact with films, none of us drank alcohol or even smoked cigarettes.

My first romantic experience involved neither Marta nor Danka, but rather a nice Jewish girl. Her name was Bella, or affectionately Belusia. She was a pretty brunette, a little younger than me, and from a very devout family in town. First, we saw each other among a group of friends and then we started having individual dates. When things had gotten serious enough, I went to her home and met her mother. Belusia and I talked seriously about politics, books, music, and art. And I, older and more experienced, got to feel like a man of the world. Our best dates ended at the Soła Beach, where we kissed and petted.

As night fell on the Soła, we gathered our things and turned for home. The river's banks provided a perfect view of the town, whose ancient and modern buildings were jumbled together in a complexity of civil, military, and religious institutions. Farthest off to the left was the tower of the Piast Fortress, next on the right came the Silesian monastery, the Great Synagogue, and in the foreground, the post office and courthouse. Walking home we talked about our plans and prospects. Our own futures, of course, remained veiled and hidden, and no one could imagine what was to come for the community stretched out before us: Oświęcim, which the Germans called Auschwitz, was just a town like any other.[9]

The *matura* exam would make or break me, or so it seemed at the time. Part oral, part written, comprising every major subject we had studied, the test was a major obstacle to educational advancement. Failing it would be humiliating, but an even worse stigma was attached to those who didn't take it at all.

My brother, Tadek, had never been an excellent student. Sixteen-years-old when our father died, the tragedy seemed to have completely derailed his academic journey. His grades slipped. Nothing mother could say had any effect. He dropped out of gymnasium before the exams and took a job in a factory that manufactured tarpaper for roofing. He may or may not have enjoyed the work, but he probably liked it more than attending classes, and he had plans someday to learn the finer points of his profession at a vocational school in France. But this didn't satisfy the family, which I have no doubt, put enormous pressure on Tadek to stick with his studies. With us, school counted for everything, and in the weeks leading up to my *matura*, I worked harder than ever before to get my lessons perfect.

I felt confident. While my classmates crammed desperately, I only needed to refresh my memory. After eight disciplined and focused years, I had a strong grasp of the material. That's not to say I slept easily in May 1937 as the test approached. But when it was finished, and I had sweated through the oral interrogations of the examiners, I knew that I had done well. My grades were mostly "A," with a "B" in math. My path to university was clear. As a reward, my family paid for me to travel to Vienna for the summer to stay with my father's family. The trip would be a vacation, a carefree interlude before I began university in the fall.

I was familiar with my mother's family, but not with that of my father. From the very beginning of my trip, I felt like I was communing with Zarnowitzes, past and present. To get my passport to Austria, I first needed to travel to Zator to obtain some documents. I walked from Oświęcim, hitching rides on peasant carts when I could. The small town of Zator was where my father had been born. My grandfather, the Hebrew scribe, had lived and died there, and after I had picked up the paperwork I needed, I visited his grave in the ancient Jewish cemetery.

Then I was ready to travel. The train steamed west, crossing the Polish border into Czechoslovakia. I was eighteen years old and this was the first time I had ever left the country. My *matura* exam was behind me and university loomed ahead. I had some zlotys in my pocket and I felt like an adult. From Brno, the train turned south, passed into Austria, and with a final lurch, braked in Vienna's East Station.

My father's family was there to show me the city. We crossed the Danube Canal and entered the old neighborhood of Leopoldstadt, which had such a high percentage of Jewish inhabitants that it was known as *Mazzesinsel*, or Matzos Island. There, on Hollandstrasse, my uncle Heinrich and aunt Kamilla lived in an apartment above their fur shop. Heinrich, my father's older brother, had sacrificed his own academic dreams to open a business and support his two siblings in their studies. At the time of my visit, both of their daughters were gone. Ella, the eldest, had been recently married to Fred Wind, a businessman. The younger daughter, Trudy, married Max Guth, whose family owned the large Hotel Guth on a nearby street in

Leopoldstadt. Both of these young families were vacationing in the Italian Alps.

My third uncle, Simon, the youngest brother, had become a prosperous life-insurance lawyer. He convinced me that I should follow his example and study the law at university.

But that was still a few months off. In the meantime, I could explore one of the most cosmopolitan and beautiful cities of Europe. I walked everywhere, visiting the famous sights and museums. I heard and saw superb singers, notably Ezio Pinza and Elisabeth Rethberg, in Verdi's *Aida* and *La Forza del Destino*, as well as Gounod's *Faust*, in the Staatsoper, Vienna's great opera house. I also saw the Karl Marx Hof, an ultramodern three-quarters-of-a-mile-long housing development that had been constructed by the Socialist government in 1930. Built for workers, the complex featured kindergartens and communal gardens. In 1934, a fascist counterrevolution had driven the Leftists from power. A pitched battle had been fought over the apartment block, and when I visited three years later, the bullet holes were still there to see, memorials to the city's troubled past.[10]

And, of course, there were troubles in the present, too. In the three years that followed the counterrevolution, Austrian chancellor Dollfuss had been assassinated. The state police had put down numerous revolts by both Socialist and Nazi factions. The new chancellor had grown weaker while Hitler's forces had strengthened. By the time I visited the city, sentiment had definitely swung toward the Nazis. Disaster was looming, the signs all showed it. And yet, it was easier to hope for a cure than to imagine the full extent of the disease. A joke circulating in the summer of 1937 described the situation in Vienna as "hopeless but not serious."[11]

I was unable to see into the future and so spent a pleasant trip. I left in the early autumn, bidding an easy adieu to my relatives, promising to see them again soon, and looking forward to the next phase in my life, studying law at Kraków University.

■ ■ ■

Still living at home in Oświęcim, I commuted to university in Kraków, which was a little more than an hour away. This arrangement saved money on housing, but meant early mornings and late nights, leaving at dawn and returning after dark. On the trains, I studied or slept. Though I remained under my mother's roof, I had ventured beyond the protection of my family for the first time. Kraków University was Europe in a microcosm. When I entered as a first-year law student in the autumn of 1937, the campus—like the continent—was in absolute turmoil. Finally, I began to feel the truth of my status as a Jew in Poland.

Throughout the 1930s, the Socialists, Communists, and Fascists had struggled for dominance over the globe, for streets, and in classrooms. In Poland, the conflict was often between Jews and non-Jews, or as it was more commonly delineated: Jews and Poles. In 1929, Kraków University had been shut down for six months after student factions skirmished with each other in organized street fights. The Poles burned yarmulkes, and darkly demanded that the number of Jewish medical students equal the number of Jewish corpses supplied for dissection.[12]

Anti-Semitism was the official, though unstated, policy of the universities. A quota—called the *numerus clausus*—was established on the number of Jewish students who could enroll in certain programs. The strictest limits were set on the professional degrees. In medicine, there was basically *numerus nullus*—no Jews allowed. In my law school, there were at most two dozen Jews in a class of several hundred students. But even this was too much for Polish fascists of the National Democratic, or Endek, Party.

The Endeks had been around for more than a decade. In 1932, when violence had broken out at the universities, they had barred Jewish students from entering the classrooms in Warsaw, shouting "Beat the Jews, and screw their girls!"[13] Gaining strength and inspiration from the rise in Hitler's power, they thought that we Jews were a bigger threat to Poland than the increasingly militaristic Nazis. "Germany's success," an Endek paper declared, "teaches us in Poland to adopt the same policy, which will force the Jews to organize their own mass emigration. We can do that only by making the Jews realize once and for all that there will be no stopping until not a single Jew is left in Poland."[14]

The National Democratic students at Kraków tried to bully us into sitting in the back of a lecture hall, but on the whole we succeeded in resisting it. However, once or twice a semester, they called for a "Day Without Jews." Signs would be hung around campus in advance, and then on the morning in question the fascists would stand by the gates in packs, stopping us from attending our classes. When this happened,

I would just turn around and go home. Sometimes the Polish students who belonged to the Leftist groups would fight with the Endeks. But I felt trapped in the middle, with little chance to help. So, I still tried to focus on my studies. The Jews were overwhelmingly outnumbered, and we were too weak.

On a frigid winter morning, during my first year, I got on the train at sunrise and rode to school. I was one of the first students to arrive at the aula, the largest lecture hall on campus. I hung my winter coat from a hook on the wall and took my seat in a row toward the front. The course, Roman Law, was mandatory for all first-year students. We were studying the courts and penal codes of the ancient Romans. Our professor, Rafał Taubenschlag, was an acknowledged international authority, a member of the Papal Academy of Sciences, and a Jew. He hadn't arrived yet, but my classmates had by now filled up most of the remaining seats.

Then, there was a commotion at the door, and several Endeks entered the aula. All the students looked up to see what was happening. My heart sank.

"Today is a day without Jews," they announced, "and all the Jews must leave the room!" Without using violence, they used the threat of violence to make their point clear: you are absolutely not allowed to stay. From around the lecture hall, the other Jews stood, gathered their things, and started to head for the doors. I joined them, picking my way carefully, and with as much composure as I could maintain, through the row and down the aisle. I could feel hundreds of eyes burning into me, and most of them felt cold and unsympathetic. It was the most humiliating moment of my life. One of my persecutors had attended my gymnasium in Oświęcim. He had even dated Danka, the Polish beauty, my first crush.

I was not even allowed to retrieve my winter coat. All morning I stood outside in the freezing chill. Why us? Why the Jews? Why me? My father had been a loyal servant of the state. My family had been of modest means. I had a patriotic attachment to a strong and free Poland. It seemed obvious to me that Jewish and non-Jewish Poles were allies against the same threats: the Soviets and Nazis. But the Endeks, and the silent anti-Semites, had been taught that it was the Jews, especially those who had the gall to study with them, that were the principal enemies of Poland. It was the saddest thing.

Some nights, when I studied late with my friends, I would remain in Kraków rather than make the tedious journey home. We had little money for eating out or seeing shows, so usually we stayed in the dormitories. Gathering in the students' rooms, we analyzed the international situation. After years of increasingly ominous threats, but little action, things were beginning to happen quickly.

In my second term, during the spring of 1938, Austrian Nazis overthrew their own government. Hitler's troops entered the country without meeting any opposition, and the *Anschluss*, or annexation, of Austria into Germany was a fait accompli. Vicious crowds swarmed through Leopoldstadt, the Jewish section of Vienna where I had stayed with my uncle the previous year, and forced any Jews they met to crawl on the streets and scrub the pavement. "Who has found work for the Jews?" they sneered at their toiling victims, "Adolf Hitler."

My uncle Heinrich—that good-natured, cultured man—was among the first of the Austrian Jews to be sent to Dachau. Only his ashes came back, along with a note saying he'd died of "heart failure." Luckily, the rest of my Viennese family took the hint, and was able to flee to New York.

Hitler had gradually marshaled his strength. For years, he had steadily advanced, while England and France had given way before him. But with the *Anschluss*, everything exploded. At the end of September 1938, England and France failed to take a stand at the Munich conference. Two months later, on November 9–10, 1938, the *Kristallnacht*, an organized pogrom, was perpetrated across Germany. Czechoslovakia was dismembered in March 1939.

These events made my second year in Kraków worse than my first. Our late night conversations grew increasingly pessimistic. The Endeks became more brazen. Hitler began demanding that territories added to Poland in the Versailles Treaty—particularly the Baltic port of Danzig—be returned to the Reich. England advised Poland's leaders not to attempt to prepare for war, upgrade the military, or in any way provoke a German response.

For as long as we could, we denied the fact that Poland would be the next step in the Nazi's march. Then, in late August 1939, the world learned of the Hitler–Stalin Pact. Our two ancient enemies had promised not to attack one another. A provision of the treaty calling for the division of Poland between the two powers was kept secret, but we hardly needed to read the fine print to comprehend the general picture. The Polish army at last began to mobilize, but it was far too late.

To create a pretense for invasion, Nazi propagandists claimed that Poles had committed atrocities against Germans. When that was unconvincing, they dredged up their ancient right to Danzig. Internally, they justified an attack in racist terms; after all, the Poles were *untermenschen*, inferior people, just a little better than the Jews. Twelve prisoners from Buchenwald were poisoned, dressed in Polish uniforms, and shot. The bodies were then planted near the border town of Gliwice. This charade allowed Hitler to tell the Reichstag that Poland had invaded Germany—with twelve soldiers—and that the German response—with a million soldiers and thousands of tanks and planes—was simply a matter of self-defense.

Luftwaffe bombers flew sorties over Kraków, Katowice, Warsaw, and our other major cities. The German Army crossed the border into Poland on several fronts. It was just before dawn on September 1, 1939.

17 Days

3 ■ ■ ■ In August 1939, workers and students were returning to routine after vacation, while the weather continued unusually warm. Some of the talk was of the usual sort: catching up, swapping stories about travel and adventure. However, the impending crisis could not be ignored. The newspapers put out extra editions, telling of the latest diplomatic maneuvers, and the copies sold out quickly.[1]

"It is impossible to describe the sense of coming explosion," Sir Evelyn Wrench, a British traveler noted in his diary. "I only hope the Poles are as ready as they say they are, and that they are not under-estimating their foe." In Danzig, he saw holiday crowds "indulging in sun-bathing and jazzing as if Nazism did not exist." In Warsaw, the citizens' behavior was almost too calm. "If anything, they have adopted too readily a policy of 'Business as usual,'" Wrench noted. "There was not anything in the way of trenches or bombproof shelters near Warsaw, and no gas masks had been issued."[2]

There was a fraternal feeling in the streets of Kraków. Strangers strategized and commiserated. We all felt the common threat and rallied together, but I had not forgotten my mistreatment at the hands of the anti-Semitic students. I was nearly twenty years old, and the "Day Without Jews" had finally dispelled my illusions about my country. Growing up in a patriotic household with assimilated parents, I had considered myself a Pole first, and then a Jew (when I had made the distinction at all). But lately I had learned that in the eyes of many of my countrymen, I would always be just a Jew: a member of a despised minority. Nevertheless, I decided that if there was to be a war, then I would find a way to join the army as a volunteer. I didn't want to see Poland defeated. Even the anti-Semitic Poles were better than the Nazis.

At the last minute, the people of Kraków finally began to take necessary precautions. Until then, afraid of provoking the Germans, we had made almost no preparations for war. On the final day of August 1939, civilians rushed to gather sand from the beaches to reinforce air-raid shelters. They dug trenches and stored the valuable collections of museums and libraries. Around noon, placards announcing a national military call-up were posted on city walls. People clustered to read them. Men with mobilization cards said goodbye to their families, gathered their belongings, and left to join their units. That night, volunteers circulated through the streets, making sure that all the windows were blacked out.[3]

There was no question of commuting to Kraków for classes on Friday, September 1, 1939. The University was closed, and the taxis and trains had all been requisitioned for use by the army.[4] I stayed at home with my mother, my grandmother, and my brother, Tadek. The women, having already survived a world war two decades earlier, were better prepared than my brother and I who had never experienced such an upheaval. But, none of us knew what to expect. There was nothing productive to be done. We relied on the government and the army to protect us, but no one had much faith in their ability to do so.

We stayed indoors and listened to the radio, hoping for news. Nazi antennae in Breslau spat hate-filled propaganda in heavily accented Polish.[5] Our stations broadcast military marches, national folk songs, and mazurkas. The government cut in with updates: bombers had attacked several cities, contact had been made with the enemy. The announcements were generally optimistic, and we wanted desperately to believe them. Sometimes, the music was interrupted by strange messages. "Attention!" a voice would shout, "Here is Charles, point 16 has just passed— chocolate—chocolate—C.F. coming—paper." Coded messages such as this one were being sent by observers at the front to warn of incoming enemy planes.[6]

When the war arrived, it would quickly overwhelm Oświęcim, just thirty miles away from the border of Greater Germany. Several times that first morning, I heard Nazi squadrons speeding overhead. A few bombs fell on the town, killing civilians on their way to work.[7] Our position was far from secure. The railroad station—a crucial junction in the middle of one of Poland's most industrialized regions—was a short walk from our house. The region was rich in iron, zinc, lead, and salt deposits. Soon, the Nazis would be coming our way.

The whole town was on edge. Without official orders or instructions, we were vulnerable to rumors and confusion. Any impetus could push us off into panic, and it wasn't long in coming. Before the first day ended, our neighbors watched in dismay as the Polish army—our sole defenders—passed through town and fled toward the interior. Wounded, shell-shocked, and disheartened, the soldiers hurried down the streets of Oświęcim without looking around, intent on moving on. Mixed in with the soldiers, were civilian refugees from the border towns. It was shocking to realize that these homeless, fearful wanderers had been—that very morning—people just like us. Most were Jews, their towns had been sacked, and they were in flight. This was happening. And, before long, it would be happening to my family.

The next day was *Shabbos* (Saturday is Shabbos, Jewish day of rest). Many of the Jewish citizens of Oświęcim awoke that morning and felt the same impulse: flee. The Germans were coming. They were almost here. No time to carefully pack. No time to clearly divide what would be helpful on the roads from what would be a burden. We took random things, often the wrong things. We gathered all the money in the house, and we left. I forget exactly what we carried, but I know that it was too little for what we would need, and too much for what we could actually bear. The only clothes I had were the ones I was wearing. I brought one treasured heirloom, a valuable Swiss Schaffhausen wristwatch that had belonged to my father.

My mother and grandmother, Tadek and I, left Oświęcim and began to walk east. We had no plan or destination. Logic was not involved. In the short term, staying at home would no doubt have been a safer course for us. But we fled, and hundreds of thousands of others did the same.

In its long history, Poland had scored some glorious victories but also sustained some spectacular defeats. The nation's level plains and indefensible borders had made it the most invaded land in Europe. But centuries before these invasions at last succeeded, Polish knights had ranked among the strongest in Christendom, and less than twenty years had passed since Marshal Pilsudski and his cavalry had routed Stalin's Red Army.

But on this occasion some Poles were too proud of their military heritage. "We are the people to whom the Prussians once gave homage," a top commander had growled a few months before the war began. If Germany invaded, he swore, the mailed fist of Poland would "fall on the head of the enemy and level him with the dust." Not all Polish generals were living in the past. "While not as great as the German Army," commander-in-chief Edward Rydz-Śmigły had said, the Polish army, "is still a good army." Even that lukewarm pronouncement would prove a bit optimistic.

The Poles knew they lacked the wealth and technology of their enemies, but they counted on the faith and strength of the people. After centuries of servitude, the nation had enjoyed only two decades of independence. "We have learnt from experience what it means to live without freedom," Rydz-Śmigły said, "and we are ready to die rather than lose it again."[8] In the preceding years, Britain and France, Austria and Czechoslovakia, had all yielded to Hitler without a fight. But Poland would not.

Hitler's invasion began at 4:45 a.m. on the morning of September 1, 1939, when 80 percent of Germany's frontline infantry units—fifty-two divisions in all—crossed the border.[9] On paper, the two armies were numerically similar, each numbering around 1.5 million men. But Poland had not fully mobilized, and was so underequipped that it could not even supply rifles to all of its soldiers.

From 1933 to 1939, nearly half of Poland's annual budget had gone to the military, an outrageous burden for an impoverished state.[10] But it was all a waste. Germany, a far richer country, had spent thirty times as much, and those resources had been disbursed more effectively. The Nazis had built a modern army and were using it. Their attack was spearheaded by all seven of their tank divisions, and all eight divisions of motorized infantry. The open plains of our country were ideal for tank maneuvers, and the unusually hot weather had left the ground firm and dry. The Polish military, which had always relied with pride on horsemanship, faced the Nazis with only two tank brigades, but eleven brigades of cavalry.

As the tanks clattered over the earth, almost the entire Luftwaffe—roughly 2,000 planes of all types—winged ahead. Bombs fell on Warsaw and Katowice. It was still dark when the first raiders arrived over Kraków. Slipping into a dive, the pilots sighted the Polish airfields at the edge of town. In minutes, the hangars were reduced to twisted beams and rubble.[11] The Polish air force had roughly 400 flyable aircraft. Its obsolete fighters were too slow to even engage the enemy's bombers, but it hardly mattered. Most of its planes were destroyed on the ground in the first minutes of fighting.[12]

The Germans were launching a double pincer movement, striking simultaneously at the north and south. The attack combined unstoppable mass with unheard-of precision: it was the *Blitzkrieg*. The Nazis had first practiced it in Spain, now they were perfecting it in Poland. The main thrust came through the "Moravian Gate" toward Silesia. There were 886,000 soldiers in this army group, along with artillery and armor, fighters and bombers, mobile kitchens and command centers, fuel suppliers and mechanics—and the whole enterprise was aimed directly toward the south-west corner of Poland where we lived.

We had no plan, except to keep away from the Nazis. So we went east, toward Zator, fourteen miles away. I had taken this same old and well-traveled road two years earlier. That had been a tranquil, pleasant day in the countryside. Now, the path was jammed.

A refugee on a nearby road that day described the scene of exodus:

Private cars, taxis and lorries tried to force their right of way by using their loudest horns, hooting incessantly. Horse-drawn carriages of all kinds, from buggies and hansoms to heavy wagons, went nearer the two edges of the road. Cyclists and motor-cyclists, riding at top speed, tried to weave their way among the slower-moving traffic. The crowd of pedestrians, pushed off the road, strove relentlessly on, filling the gaps between vehicles and slowing down their progress.[13]

I wish I could say we were brimming with compassion, or that we shared a feeling of togetherness, but it quickly became obvious that people were just concerned with the good of themselves and their families. The fraternal feeling that some noticed before the war had not lasted once the guns began to fire. Instead of marching together in a single mass, we were divided into little groups. We were headed in the same direction, but we were by no means all going there together. We didn't make friends on the way. There was not much conversation. When a peasant cart went by, we all competed for a spot on board. A few times we were lucky and my mother and grandmother got a seat.

We were afraid of the Germans. All the Jews in Poland knew to fear them, but few, at this early date, knew as much as we did about Nazi atrocities. We had family in Austria. My uncle had died in Dachau. The threat of them had forced us out of our homes. It kept us marching. But even we probably didn't fear them as much as we should have. The truth about Hitler was more terrible than we could imagine. So, I remember on that first day, a lingering spirit of adventure, especially for me and my brother. There was no work or school. We had no precedent for what we were experiencing. Despite the general anxiety, there was a hint of holiday in the air.

We kept hoping to see some sign of the Polish army. The fighting was not going our way—that we could tell—but we assumed that the initial retreat had been just a temporary setback. At any moment, we expected to come across the new defensive line. Assuming that this war would proceed as the last one had, we thought in terms of trenches and battles of attrition. However, we never saw any of our soldiers. Instead, we heard the ominous sound of enemy artillery, pounding away, too close for comfort.

Hitching a ride was a rare luxury, and for the most part, we walked. Tadek and I were in our everyday clothes. I don't remember if we had umbrellas, coats, or even hats, but it was too hot for those things anyway. Even lightly dressed, we were sweating. Before long it became obvious that the women were slowing us down. My grandmother was an old woman, and my mother was well on into middle age. Other groups were moving faster than we were. It was frustrating to see them pass. If we were to escape the enemy, every minute and every mile would count.

At the end of a long day, we finally reached the small town of Zator. During my previous visit, I had taken the time to visit my grandfather's gravestone. On Sept. 2, 1939, no one had the luxury of thinking about the past. Our present was all that mattered, and it was obvious that the women could go forward no longer.

Then, our worst fears were realized. A group of German soldiers were just across the river Skawa, in plain sight. They wore green uniforms, and watched us through binoculars. From that distance, they didn't seem particularly menacing. They looked confident and calm, their timetable was proceeding smoothly and on schedule. Some tanks and armored troop transports droned in the background. A group of officers stood talking, probably planning the best way to cross the river and occupy the next objective.

We had not expected to see the Germans so soon and so close. The implications were clear. Oświęcim must have fallen already. They were here. They had won. Our situation, which had seemed hazy and uncertain, suddenly snapped into focus. The women realized this first. They fell back for a few moments and discussed something between themselves. When they rejoined us, they had already made the decision. They were presenting us with a conclusion, not asking us to make a choice. They were turning around.

The four of us stood together and held a huddled meeting on the shoulder of the road outside of town. We can't go on, they told us. We're going home. We'll live quietly in our own house. The Nazis won't bother us: two old women, both of whom speak fluent German. We'll be fine. But, you two must go on. You're Jewish men of military age, and things would be very bad for you under the occupation.

They had nobly made this choice for us, knowing that we couldn't have done so on our own. They knew our only hope was to push on without them. We didn't try to change their minds. Even after a single day it was clear that they were right, and we had many hard days of walking ahead of us. They were holding us back and we were eager to get along. They gave us most of the money. We hugged and kissed them. We didn't know when we would get another chance to embrace them. We thought it could be months, or even years, but still it was a hurried farewell with few tears shed. Tadek and I pushed forward, toward Kraków. They turned to struggle against the current of the fleeing masses, retracing their weary steps back to the family home. Not for a single moment did I suspect that it was the last time I would ever see them.

We separated on the evening of September 2, 1939. I don't remember where, or even if, Tadek and I slept that night. At most, we might have rested under the stars for a few hours. Early Sunday morning we were on the road again. Now that it was just the two of us, we were determined to cover as much ground as possible. We were fit and experienced hikers. A few years earlier, we had gone on a summer backpacking trip through the Carpathian Mountains in southern Poland. Compared to that strenuous climbing, this was just a stroll along a flat, well-traveled road. We put the miles behind us. Our next goal was Kraków, and we were not even halfway there yet.

This was only the third day of war. We were still in Poland. It was in Polish that people were speaking all around us. Our zlotys retained their value and we could use them to buy meals. But, there was no sign of the government: no policemen, no officials. It was impossible to get a newspaper, and our information arrived in the form of rumors that rippled up and down the road, seeping from group to group.

The Nazis were behind us—we didn't know how far. They were in vehicles and we were on foot. But we were in headlong flight, while they had to move with caution, deal with lingering resistance, and consolidate their supply lines. Those factors seemed to even the odds, and we imagined that if we kept moving at top speed, we might maintain our slim margin of safety. But that hope vanished when the Stukas came.

The birds were the first to sense the approaching threat; they circled nervously in the sky. Then the horses reared their heads, and the dogs pulled at their ropes. Finally, the engines became audible to the refugees on the road. We ran to find some cover, cowering behind trees or leaping into ditches. It was a fatal mistake to hide beneath a cart, because the horses would bolt, and the wheels could mutilate the people below.

The Nazi airmen dropped down to a few feet off the ground, swaying the treetops as they came. Their bullets strafed the defenseless crowds. It was murder, sickeningly simple to commit. "The machine-gun fire was generally well aimed," a Polish survivor recalled. "The pilot, flying safely and very low, could see perfectly well every one of us and aim his weapon at every large group that he noticed. Of the hundreds of bullets, a few score would find their targets." When they were finally gone, we climbed out of our hiding places and looked around. Dead bodies lay scattered across the road.[14]

We reached Kraków late Monday. Here we hoped to rest, but we learned that the city was undefended and nearly empty. The Jewish neighborhood, Kazimierz, was deserted. German bombers attacked several times a day, and the enemy land forces were closing in. We obviously weren't safe here. The railroad station, which I had passed through morning and night during my entire time at university, had been attacked by incessant air raids. We had hoped to catch a train in the city, but in the end, we didn't even bother trying—the crowds would be unbearable. Instead, having wasted precious hours of our slim lead, we passed through town, and pressed on through Tuesday.[15]

To the east of Kraków, the crowds were thicker than before. From a city of almost a quarter-million inhabitants, at least one-third, or 75,000, had taken to the roads.[16] Vehicles passed us, sending up clouds of dust.

A railroad line, heading for the distant city of Lwów, ran parallel to the road, and the passing trains offered a tantalizing means of salvation. But they were full to bursting, with desperate passengers sitting on the roofs and clinging to the outsides of the doors.

At a minor village depot, we found a train idling in the station. Like the others, it was jammed with people. We searched from the front to the back without success. We were ready to give up, when we found an empty spot above the last car. It was an observation post usually occupied by workers, but somehow on this day it was empty. Tadek and I climbed into our little perch on top of the caboose. The locomotive puffed and started pulling, and we were on our way. Almost immediately, we dropped into a serene sleep, our first real rest in four days.

I was being swept along in one of history's epic retreats. But that, in and of itself, was not necessarily bad news for Poland. None but the most jingoistic or deluded had believed the army could stand toe-to-toe against the Germans. The generals' plan had always called for a strategic abandonment of the country's western provinces.

Falling back slowly and in good order, the army would annoy the invaders with little pockets of defense, harass their lines of communication, and do anything possible to stall and delay their advance. Husbanding military resources, herding as many supplies and assets as possible, the Polish army would withdraw behind the country's only natural defenses — the rivers Vistula and (further east) Bug.

Having thus surrendered three-quarters of the nation's soil, the government would then hold this impregnable position for a few months, by which time the Allies would have launched their own attacks from the west. Facing every German leader's nightmare — a two-front war — Hitler would be forced to transfer his forces to the other end of Europe. The Polish army would then counterattack, triumphantly reclaiming its lost territories, en route to marching on Berlin.

That was the vision conceived by generals in peacetime. In practice, it was rendered irrelevant on the first morning of the war. The plan called for retreat, and retreat we did. But not in the gradual, well-ordered manner that the commanders had foreseen. The Nazis came on too fast and the Poles fell back in chaos. The border was overrun in hours, and even the invaders were incredulous at the weak and slapdash defenses: a single ribbon of trench, and beyond it — nothing.[17] They came on in a rush, before the Polish army could even flee. Entire divisions were trapped and forced to surrender.

Cities and towns fell by the dozen. "Behind the front," reported an eyewitness, "farm after farm, village after village, is in flames. Where shops are still intact long lines of Poles stand before them waiting for food. Other civilians search for their lost possessions among heaps of ashes and refuse." Behind the German army came the Hitler Youth to repair the damage. "Under their charge long rows of aged Jews with black beards and in astrakhan hats are seen at work in the streets. Often they have no picks or shovels and have to dig with their bare hands."[18]

The plan to retreat had disastrous consequences. It was hardly comforting for the inhabitants of the lost provinces to know that their homes had been surrendered to the Nazis in the interest of some grand strategy. To minimize our knowledge of what was happening, the government gave out no directives or instructions, and almost no information.

What news we did receive was patently false. On September 3, an official Polish communiqué declared that two German armored columns had been destroyed in Silesia. In fact, most of Silesia was already under Nazi control. Another announcement that day claimed that sixty-four Luftwaffe aircraft had been downed, compared to only eleven losses for the Polish Air Force. In fact, the Nazi claim was much closer to the truth: one hundred twenty Polish planes destroyed with just twenty-one German losses.[19] In the opening days of the war, it was impossible to get honest news from the government.

Our leaders had expected quick, decisive action from the allies, but they received nothing of the sort. England and France wasted precious days in doomed diplomatic talks, before declaring war on September 3, 1939. Even then, though most of Hitler's army was occupied, they made no attempt to strike on his exposed flank.[20] The entire strategy hinged on allied aid, but there was no sign that help was coming. Having exhausted material means, the Polish high commanders were reduced to prayer. Mostly, they prayed for rain, remembering how a storm in 1809 had trapped Napoleon's invading army in knee-deep mud. Instead, they got clear skies and no rain; the planes continued flying, and the tanks rolled on.

The whole front, hundreds of miles wide, had been transformed into a deadly race. The Polish army, and refugees like me, retreated, while the

Germans pursued us without mercy. The world's newspapers printed maps showing their progress, and every morning the shaded areas representing captured territory bloomed larger, while the unoccupied section wilted away. On September 4, the government fled Warsaw. Over the following several weeks, the seat of power would move again and again, always further east. One could picture the entire weight of the nation tilting that way, as men, vehicles, food, and supplies—pushed by the Nazis—all raced to cross the Vistula.

On September 5, Kraków fell and Germans cut off the road to Lwów.[21] Tadek and I must have been among the last to use that means of escape. By the September 14, Gdansk had been captured and Warsaw was besieged. Silesia was in enemy hands.[22] All of the nation's resources had been ordered east, even policemen, firefighters, and local officials. This left a void in the abandoned territories, where no hint of authority remained to keep the public order. These blunders of the Polish high command helped to convert a bad situation into a hopeless debacle.

By the middle of September 1939, Paris acknowledged that the Polish front had disintegrated.[23] The British high command began making plans for a war in which its ally played no part. "It is apparent," wrote the chiefs of staff in London, "that the military defeat of Poland may be accomplished in the very near future."[24]

■ ■ ■

Tadek and I rattled across southern Poland in our aerie above the caboose. The train stood still more often than it moved, and we slept more often than we were awake. In fits and starts, we trundled on. The trip from Kraków to Łańcut, ordinarily a matter of a few hours, stretched on for more than a day. Other trains on the line were bombed by German aircraft. When the passengers ran to escape the attack, the pilots would drop down and machine-gun them as they fled. We were lucky and escaped with delays, but no danger.

We were reluctant to abandon our lucky position on the caboose, but we thought it would be best to detrain at Łańcut station. At no other place in Poland were we more likely to receive shelter and information. This was my birthplace, and I still had ties to the old town. The narrow streets were unchanged, but we found no one able to help us. The Jewish section was nearly empty.

Finally, we came to our old home on Sienna Street, across from the great stables of the castle. We knocked on the door and were received by Marysia, our neighbors' Polish maid, who had been a benevolent and maternal fixture in my childhood. Alone in the house, she did everything she could for us. But in Łańcut, as elsewhere, the feeling was that the Germans were closing in. We could not stay.

Marysia saw us out, and before we left to renew our march, she said, "It was terrible when your father died, and you boys so young, but perhaps it was better for him that he did not live to see this." Poland's suffering had just begun, but this kindly woman foresaw the terrible times that lay ahead.

The next few days bleed together in my memory. In outline, they were similar to those that went before. Still, we headed east. Still, the Nazis rushed behind us, sometimes closer, sometimes more distant, but never far. "After the first week of war," another refugee recalled, "Poland was plunged into uncertainty. No one, absolutely no one, knew what was actually happening. Perhaps the Government and the General Staff had some information, but they never shared it with the public. There was no Press, no normal communication."[25] And if the high command had no access to good intelligence, the people on the road were utterly at a loss. The only time I saw German soldiers had been that day at Zator, but their presence remained a constant threat.

The tenor of our journey had changed; any note of a holiday was long silenced. Life on the road was also different. There were no longer any automobiles—those were far ahead by now. No one gave much thought to their clothes or appearance. Hair was unkempt. Shirts were covered in dirt, or even blood. Tadek and I had come from the far side of the country, almost 100 miles away, but others had come further. We saw some who had been forced out of their homes in Czechoslovakia in March. These unfortunate nomads had been fleeing Hitler for months, they had come hundreds of miles, and yet there was no end in sight for their journey. All that walking, and still the blitzkrieg nipped at their heels.

We were always in a mass of humanity, but the individual pieces changed constantly, as people dropped out or turned around. On the first day of the war, I had noticed a chill between groups on the road. A week or so later, the crowds were even more inward looking. We made no friends and communicated little with those around us. I guess everyone had reasons to keep silent; I know we did. Even in September 1939, with the enemy no longer a vague menace but an actual danger, there were people around us who preferred a Nazi to a Jew. Many Poles saw Hitler's anti-Semitism as the bright side of the German occupation. We didn't want people to know who we were. We didn't find any companions, and we didn't talk to strangers. We remained anonymous, and we flew.

My brother and I made a good team. Through our wit, perseverance, and luck, we had made it this far. Tadek was twenty-six, and his age made him the natural leader. He made the decisions and I don't remember disagreeing with the choices he picked. We were too tired and hungry for joking around. All the energy that we could muster was spent moving on and figuring the strength and means to continue. How to find a spot on a passing cart; where to look for a berth on a crowded train? Tadek was good at dealing with this, and I hope that I was too.

The warm weather held, and for us this was a blessing, despite any aid it may have given the invaders. If we couldn't find lodgings, we slept out at night. Thousands of others did the same, or rested in barns and haystacks. Our supply of zlotys had lasted us this far and we remained able to pay for food. This was by far the greatest physical exertion of my life, but I seemed to be meeting the challenge. I was young and hopeful, and incapable of seeing the full extent of what was happening.

Having covered more than 200 miles in two weeks, we arrived in Lwów, a major city in far-eastern Poland. It may have been a milestone in our journey, but clearly it could not be our destination. Yet again, the Germans were closing in, and there was no security here. We had no choice but to move on, and we were running out of places to go. The Soviet border was less than a hundred miles to the east. If the Polish army didn't make a stand here, then our journey would have been wasted, and all hope gone.

By September 13, German tanks were on the outskirts of Lwów. The defending garrison fought off the attackers, while women and children piled up obstacles in the streets.[26] Similar scenes were being enacted in other towns around the country; the situation was as grim as could be. Warsaw, surrounded, was facing constant shelling and bombardment.[27] Human losses had been catastrophic. The invaders held more than half the country. The Polish army had retreated and retreated, but parts of it still remained intact.

The Germans had pushed so far, so fast, that they had even outrun their own supplies. Some Panzer divisions ran out of gas and became easy targets against an air attack, even an obsolete plane could destroy an

This map shows Poland in its present, i.e. post-World War II, borders, not as it had been when I lived there from 1919 to 1939. Then, Poland did not extend in the West much beyond Katowice and Poznan—Gliwice, Wroclaw, Szczecin, and Ustka were all in Germany—but the adjoining western parts of Lithuania, Belarus, and Ukraine, including Lwow, were all in Poland.

immobilized tank. If only Poland had retained a few more of its planes, the damage could have been serious. There were other reasons to feel hopeful. A relieving army managed to fight its way to the outskirts of Warsaw. The official German communiqué for September 15, admitted encountering, "very strong and desperately resisting forces."[28] Poles seemed to be gaining minor victories in several small battles. Morale began to rise. And, finally, it had begun to rain.[29]

It was September 17, 1939, and it looked as if the tide was turning.

■ ■ ■

Tadek and I were on a country lane southeast of Lwów. A nearby correspondent from the *London Times* estimated that 10,000 vehicles and roughly 80,000 fugitives were in the area. "All day," he wrote of roads just a few miles from where we limped along, "there passed the most pitiable caravan of human sorrow and misery.... Many columns of Polish refugees are trudging to the Romanian frontier carrying small bundles of their belongings. Now and again a column will halt for half an hour owing to traffic congestion on the narrow, dusty roads, and then its members fall out and pluck sunflowers to feed on the seeds."[30]

This part of Poland—Eastern Galicia—was mostly populated by Ukrainians. We started hearing their strange, foreign language, and we knew that we were far from home. Our problem, however, wasn't the distance we had already come, though we were getting short on money and nearing exhaustion; the dilemma we had to face was where we were going. The Nazis had chased us the entire breadth of Poland and were still just a day or two behind us. Now, the Soviet Union was not so far down the road. We were running out of room.

The anti-Semitic Poles I had faced in Kraków did not mind using a number of contradictory slanders against the Jews: we were all rich, we were all weak, we were all cowards, and we were all Communists. At the moment, I was dead broke. I had proven my strength in this epic march across the nation. I still hoped to volunteer for the army to show my courage. Not that I was a hero. Thousands of others, driven by the circumstances, had done as much or more. If I was not the bravest, then at least I had shown that I was no coward. But, though I was not a Red, and had always eschewed political activism in favor of my academic studies, it was true that I felt some sympathy for socialist theories.

Most of the world's radicals looked to Moscow as a beacon and ideal, but the Polish Communists I had known were different: they were suspicious of the Russians. The two nations had been at war in recent memory. They were our next-door neighbors and we knew that the dream of a proletarian republic that had glimmered in 1917 had already been replaced with a merciless dictatorship of steel. Still, we didn't fear them like we feared the Germans and viewed the Soviets as the better option.

We neared the town of Brzeżany. Tadek had been born here in 1913, before our father had been transferred to Łańcut. The countryside was wild and ancient, thickly forested with birch trees. We hadn't seen any German soldiers since the third day of the war. It had been weeks since we had even heard their airplanes and artillery. That first wave of terror had long since been replaced by tedium and fatigue. We still walked. We knew we had to keep going. But the reasons for our flight had started to grow fuzzy.

Then, approaching us from the east, we heard singing. Not in Polish, or even in the Ukrainian of the local residents. It was Russian. First a soloist called out in his clear voice, whether as a tenor or baritone. Then the rest of the troops responded together. A small group, perhaps battalion-strength, appeared on the road. They marched in beautiful order, disciplined and haughty. They wore high boots and green uniforms. There were red stars painted on their helmets. It was the Soviets. And they were in Poland.

Tadek and I stepped aside and let them pass. In our exhausted state, we had trouble coming to terms with what we were seeing. They had no reason to be here. My first reaction was happiness: perhaps they had come to help us fight the Germans. Only one thing was clear. There was no point in pushing ahead. Our march was over.

For a few days in the middle of September, when the German advance had finally stalled, resistance if not victory had seemed possible. All of Poland's remaining strength was consolidated in a tight defensive line. Every one of its guns was facing west, aimed against the German invaders. That's when, on September 17, 1939, the Soviet Union invaded from the east, stabbing Poland in the back during its most vulnerable moment.

Two million soldiers of the workers and peasants' Red Army, as well as their tanks and planes, crossed at dozens of points along the 500-mile border. Poland could only meet them with the weakest resistance. In some areas, they advanced forty miles that first day. And everywhere, according to the Russian propaganda, the population greeted their invaders "with jubilation."[31] Actually, most Poles probably reacted, as I did, with confusion. The Soviets intentionally fostered our bewilderment. "We have come to fight the Germans in Poland," the officers called to joyful crowds of refugees. "Soviet Russia declared war on Germany this morning." Of course, this was what we wanted to hear. We were eager to believe it.

But it wasn't true.[32] On September 18, the Soviet newspaper, *Izvestia*, revealed the secret articles of the Hitler-Stalin Pact. Poland was to be partitioned again, the fourth time in less than 200 years, with Russia claiming everything east of the rivers Bug and San. "Salvation comes from the Soviet Union," Alexei Tolstoy wrote that day. "Grim, unswerving and magnanimous comes the Red Army. Our brothers beyond the border, yesterday's slaves, find that in the future they are to live prosperously and happily."[33] In truth, what happened was that the Polish nation had ceased to exist.

President Moscicki, whom I had once cheered on a state visit to Oświęcim, fled to Romania. "Not for the first time in our history we are faced with an invasion inundating our country both from the west and east," he said in a broadcast from near the border. "On every one of you today rests the duty of guarding the honor of the nation. No matter what may befall you, Almighty Providence will render justice to our cause."

Tadek and I had outrun a million Germans for more than two weeks, only to stumble headlong into two million oncoming Russians. If the two armies were arrows, as the newspaper maps depicted them, then we were exactly between them, getting poked by both points.

We turned and retraced our steps to Lwów. There was no way to know if our flight had been a failure or a success. We had made our attempt and had come farther than most. The previous three weeks had severed me from my previous life. Not only was I separated from my mother, but also every institution I had known since birth had disintegrated. There was nothing left to do but wait.

The Gulag

4 ■ ■ ■ We were not welcomed in Lwów. Hundreds, if not thousands, of refugees arrived each day, and it became increasingly difficult to find accommodations. The streets were packed, and certain neighborhoods took on the appearance of a refugee camp. For the locals, even the local Jews, there were simply too many of us (escapees).

On September 20, 1939, Tadek and I had arrived from the east in a straggling column. We were hundreds of miles from our family, isolated and abandoned. There was no one here who knew us, took any interest in us, or cared about our well-being. We rented an apartment, and though it was by no means luxurious, we soon came to feel grateful to have a roof over our heads.[1] We had a kitchen and a bathroom, with electric lights.

Our building had a wooded lot out back, but it was in a busy area, very close to the rail yards. The locomotives drove through the depot night and day. We got used to the noise, but the trains themselves became a disturbing reminder of our situation. Some cars were painted with swastikas, others with red stars. They rolled west and east, evidencing the flourishing trade that existed between our two conquerors.

Lwów became the local administrative center for the Soviet occupiers. Red Army soldiers and officers were everywhere. They crowded the streets and cafes. They had plenty of money—both zlotys and rubles were at first accepted as currency—and bought everything they could find, until the shelves in all the shops were empty.[2] I grew accustomed to the Russians, and appreciative of their behavior, which was good, or at least not bad: polite, though distant. In general, they didn't bother too much about us. They probably had been ordered to act properly and not get too close to their new subjects.

The stance of their government was different. Officially, we were the enemy. The Union of Soviet Socialist Republics (USSR) and Poland remained nominally at war. Hitler was our foe, but he and Stalin were allies. The Soviets didn't see us as harmless refugees who had fled from Nazi aggression into the eastern regions of our own country. To them, we were enemy nationals, and each of us could have been a terrorist or saboteur. Lwów was no longer part of Poland as Poland didn't exist any more. In October 1939, the newly minted district of "Western Ukraine" went to the polls for a referendum on joining the USSR. The secretary-general of the local Communist Party, Nikita Khrushchev, made sure of the results, and 91 percent were reportedly in favor of the proposal.[3] Neither Tadek nor I, nor any of the refugees from the west, were invited to vote.

Through no fault of our own, therefore, we were in Soviet territory. Moreover, we were here illegally. Our occupiers viewed us with suspicion and labeled us, in classic Communist parlance, as a "dangerous (*opasny*) element." We were presented with two choices. We could register with one bureaucracy and ask to be repatriated back to Nazi-occupied Oświęcim, or we could register with another bureaucracy, receive a "passport" and identity (ID) card, entrain for Russia, and begin new lives as Soviet citizens. This, we understood, was considered to be a very generous offer.

We had no official link with home. We had no radio. The Russian newspapers, of course, printed nothing about German atrocities, but the demarcation line remained fluid and people moved back and forth be-tween the occupied zones. We heard rumors about conditions in the west, but the reports were insubstantial and conflicting. In late November 1939, the Soviets finally opened up mail and telegraph communications to the rest of the country.[4]

We immediately sent a postcard to our family. Mother answered quickly and sent promising news. She and our grandmother were all right at home. The soldiers in Oświęcim were not Germans, but Austrians. Thinking back to the benevolent days of Austria–Hungary, we naively perceived them as more sympathetic. Finally, mother wrote that my old girlfriend, Belusia, whom I had kissed on the Soła Beach in town, had visited our house. The two had really hit it off. In all, the situation looked not so bad, and mother suggested that we return.

The thought was very appealing, and we wanted to follow her advice. But, though we sent several more postcards home, we never got another response. Meanwhile, people continued to arrive in Lwów. They were desperate to cross the border into the Russian territory, and that seemed to suggest that we were better off staying where we were. We had met several old acquaintances, and there were refugees everywhere: we became a community in movement. There was nothing to offer our friends in the little apartment, so we talked in cafés. At many tables, the same conversation was taking place: stay or go? We knew the Nazi threat—or thought we did—but the Russians were inscrutable.

We were being urged to choose a direction. The decision felt crucial and life changing, as indeed it was. We had no facts. Sentimentally, we wanted to go home, to our mother and grandmother. Tadek and I still felt very attached to our former way of life and we had a strong intuitive feeling that applying for Soviet citizenship meant abandoning all of this. On the other hand, we also still shared great fears of the Nazis.

All around us, people were choosing. German officers arrived at a villa in the suburbs and started filing applications for those who wished to return. Thousands lined up each day. The Soviets gave out registration papers, but their office was usually closed; when it was open it was hopelessly overcrowded. The border was sealed. Movement from one zone to the other ceased, and makeshift encampments sprouted on the banks of the River San. Many refugees had been trapped between the lines and were not being allowed to move in either direction.[5]

Stalin or Hitler. East or west. We had no way to choose. There was no right answer. We were paralyzed. We procrastinated. In the end, we did nothing. We didn't register for repatriation or apply for a passport. For months, we sat and waited. And, looking back, that turned out to be the best decision.

The rains that had held off in September arrived with a vengeance in October and November. In December, the zloty was devalued, and we immediately had to find paying jobs. The Russians hired us as road pavers, and paid us between four and eight rubles a day. These were nearly starvation wages, just enough to cover a loaf or two of bread, or a pint of milk. Butter, at thirty rubles a pound, was a luxury item. Meat we could not afford. As the winter continued, we tried to find coal to heat our rooms, but fuel was in short supply.[6] We labored every day to keep alive. This was hard work, unskilled, and unrewarding but, we hoped, temporary and respectable in the self-proclaimed supreme workers' state. Both of us were in good shape, proud that we managed, and grateful for being in a place apparently free of a policy of racial discrimination. At night, I listened to the seemingly endless stream of passing trains.

For nine months, we lived this life. We were powerless and inert. Our only object was to find enough work to continue paying our bills. We knew nothing about the outside world. There was no change in our situation. We were tense, but sluggish. In the spring, the warm weather brought more jobs. However, in June 1940, there was a sudden change. Rumors fired through the expatriate community: the Soviets were deporting refugees. We knew of certain actual arrests of our acquaintances. We did not know what the charges against them were. We wondered what we ourselves would face, or how we should react. The uncertainty added to our fears. One by one, people were disappearing. The soldiers came and took whole families from their apartments.

The atmosphere in Lwów grew poisoned. Since the arrests always happened at night, Tadek and I started hiding out after dark. We would crouch down among the trees in the wooded lot behind our apartment building. In the daytime, we went inside and slept. We did this for less than a week. Then, in the middle of the night, the Soviet *militia* came and found us. They trucked us to the Peter and Paul fortress, an old military barracks on a hill in the center of town. There, we were incarcerated, along with other detainees. It was a prison, though we were allowed to converse freely and roam around inside the walls. Once or twice a day, we all gathered at a long table to eat the soy beans the guards dished out. We were not charged or interrogated. We didn't know what would happen next. We simply waited.

At the end of the month, we boarded trucks and were driven toward the outskirts of town. We left behind the apartment buildings and passed single-family homes with yards and gardens. Train cars were in the distance, standing on tracks within a fenced enclosure.[7] The soldiers loaded us onto a cattle train, which had been modified for human passengers.

We sat on wooden partitions, and tried to peek through the windows that were near the ceiling of the car. Again, there was no explanation. We sat in the station for several days without moving. On the second day, our aunt Paula came and walked along the train until she spotted one of us at a window; then she stopped. We waved at each other, and she seemed to cry. Like other visitors, she must have heard about the train from private rumors. This was the first time we learned that we had family in town.

On a later day, just before the train was set to depart, I heard my name called through a loudspeaker. A guard opened the door of our car and told me to get out. Tadek moved to come, too, but he was ordered to stay. There was nothing to do but obey. I said a brief goodbye to my brother and walked off the train. All eyes followed my progress as I passed down the aisle and stepped down into the open air. Soldiers ordered me to sit in the backseat of an official car. I had no idea why they had singled me out. I examined every possible reason and circumstance. I could think of nothing that would have set me apart from my brother, or from anyone else. As far as I knew, I was totally unexceptional.

The soldiers drove me back to the Peter and Paul fortress. Surely, I thought, the time had come for an explanation. I expected, at any minute, to be taken into a dark room, placed under a blinding lamp, and subjected to the third-degree. I dreaded it, but at least the ordeal might finally bring me some answers. Anything, at this point, would have felt better than the suspense. For a week, I was treated like others. I slipped back into my former routine. I wandered the grounds and talked with other prisoners, none of whom knew anything substantial. Finally, I realized, there would be no interrogation.

Why did they separate me from my brother? It could have been a meaningless bureaucratic error, or a devilish form of psychological torture. I never found out. In either case, the mystery provided a classic lesson in Soviet policy, as relevant to the treatment of prisoners as to the organizing of an enormous planned economy. The entire enterprise was either brilliant or crazy, but you could never quite figure out which. And that was the point: uncertainty kept you docile, vulnerable, and insecure.

After a week, I was once again trucked out to the trains, exactly as before. Instead of being with my brother, I was surrounded by strangers. Perhaps, they had meant to separate us, though other families were allowed to travel together. This time, there was a much shorter wait. The locomotive gave a kick, the passengers jolted into each other, and we were off. I breathed a sigh of relief.

The train moved slowly. With about fifty people sitting inside, our car was crowded and dark. I found a seat near the window and savored the breeze. The toilet was simply a bucket on the floor. Most passengers were modest and tried to wait until dark to use it. In the daytime, people would hold up bed sheets to give some privacy.[8] We stopped often, usually on sidetracks in open fields, rather than in proper stations. Guards brought us water, kasha, and cabbage soup. We were allowed to get out and freshen up under close supervision.

There was not much conversation, but what there was, focused on a single subject: where were we going? The guards were no help. Anyone brave enough to ask them, got the inevitable answer, *Ne znaju* (I don't know). Only by standing by the window and reading the signs of the passing train stations, could we ascertain our direction. We became obsessed with it. On the day when we sighted a placard marked "Kiev," we knew that we were heading east, and were already deep inside the Soviet Ukraine. This, in itself, was good news. We had no idea where they were taking us, but at least it was not west—back into the hands of the Nazis.

I was not afraid, or appalled by my circumstances. I was worried about my brother. He and I had come too far together, I thought, to get separated so unceremoniously. But, in general, I took things as they came. Most people behaved like this. It was obvious that we were trapped in the grip of overwhelming forces. I can't say what I thought about the big picture, and saw myself as a tiny fragment in a shattered world, or that I realized I was a participant in history's greatest upheaval. It was not beyond me to think in this way, and I had many an hour to ruminate. But such thoughts seemed irrelevant at the time, as all of us were preoccupied with day-to-day survival.

After Kiev, we realized that we had changed direction and were headed north. Our journey stretched from days into weeks and the mood on the train grew more somber. Private stores of food were exhausted. People were dirty and disheveled. Most lost interest in deciphering our destination. They didn't care where we stopped, as long as we stopped soon.

I remained fascinated by the passing signs, as did another passenger, a Polish communist, who had never abandoned his optimism. Without any facts to go on, he had convinced himself that the Soviets were preparing a benign fate for us. I suddenly glimpsed the sign for "Pushkin," which, I knew from reading about the great Russian poet, had formerly been the city of Tsarskoye Seło. We were near Leningrad. Our stalwart was triumphant. This was the proof he had been waiting for. Our hosts were taking us to their greatest city. There, they would free us and provide for our needs.

But we left Leningrad far behind and continued north. Finally, the trains halted for good. The doors were opened and we stepped out into the frozen north. It was July 1940, and we were shivering. Pine, spruce, and birch trees—primordial and majestic—grew to the horizon. The natural landscape towered above a dwarfish human settlement. We saw a set of low barracks, surrounded by a wall with turrets. Everything was constructed from wood. Soon, we learned that this unimpressive and anonymous place had a name. It was a forced-labor camp in Karelia, one of the oldest and most notorious islands in Stalin's Gulag archipelago.

The chilling term "Gulag" was an acronym for the rather harmless phrase, "Main Administration of Camps."[9] The network of penal colonies had been established after the revolution of 1917, and had reached its peak once Stalin took command. Sited far away from civilian centers, in some of the least hospitable corners of the globe, the Gulag provided the Bolsheviks with penitentiaries for criminals, and a threat to hang over the heads of political enemies. As important as these functions, however, was the system's ability to supply millions of prisoners to work in places where no free laborers would go—convicts carried out many of the vast improvement schemes of the Soviet five-year plans. A memorandum from the main administration of camps put it unsentimentally: "the history of the Gulag is the history of the colonization and industrial exploitation of the remote regions of the state."[10]

One camp commandant, greeting a new batch of prisoners, put it even more simply: "You are here to work for our country, to live here and die here."[11]

Karelia, extending from the Gulf of Finland north to the White Sea at the Arctic Circle, along the border between Finland and the USSR, was about as remote as possible, this side of Siberia. It is a broad and flat land of forests and lakes, austere and frigid, but also full of its own kind of beauty. Jean Sibelius, the great Finnish composer, wrote his "Karelia" and

"Finlandia" suites in the 1890s when the territory was occupied by Tsarist Russia. His music was serene, filled with love of the countryside and its beauty.[12] For those of us who arrived as prisoners, the region spawned far graver reactions.

The earliest camp in the district had been founded in 1920 to hold the revolution's most powerful enemies. In a strange twist of fate, its construction had been ordered by the first leader of the Soviet secret service, Feliks Dzherzhinsky,[13] a close relative of my next-door neighbor in Łańcut. In the 1920s, when I lived there as a boy, speaking his name had been strictly forbidden. Arriving at the faraway camp he created, I could finally see why.

I was shown to a barrack. The simple buildings had been constructed by prison labor. They had electric lights, and were heated, barely, by wood stoves. Double bunks lined the two long walls, and I was assigned a place. I had become a Soviet prisoner, a *zaklyuchonny*, or *zek* (an inmate of a Soviet labor camp). There were two million others like me, scattered throughout the USSR, and none of us had the right to expect much good fortune.

So I was especially relieved, and also amazed, when a few days after arriving, I was trucked from the main colony to a satellite camp nearby. I was shown into a barrack, similar to the one I had seen before. And Tadek was there. Of all the brigades, throughout the vast Gulag, I had ended up in his. We had been randomly separated in Lwów, and reunited, seemingly also by chance, more than a thousand miles away. As was typical when dealing with the Soviets, it was impossible to tell whether this reunion was an unprecedented miracle, or the most natural thing in the world. In this case, I didn't care. Having my brother back was all that mattered.

In midsummer, the sky was bright well past midnight. In midwinter, darkness fell by 3:00 p.m. But, for us *zeks*, every day was the same.

An alarm bell woke us up at 6:00 A.M., and we climbed down from the feeble warmth of our beds. In the winter we usually huddled under our blankets, cocooned in all of our clothes. We had each been issued a *foofayka*, or padded vest, and a jacket, called a *koortka*, of quilted cotton. These garments made us look like medieval Russian peasants, but they kept us warm. Having washed and dressed, we ate breakfast in the dining room. This meal varied little from camp to camp. Typically it consisted of a piece of black bread, and hot oat cereal that was sometimes flavored with a little corn syrup or sunflower oil. All of our utensils—spoons, plates, and cups—were made of wood.[14]

After breakfast, our captors held the *provierka*, or roll call. Our names were shouted out, and we responded: Jewish, Polish, and Russian names. There were many of us, and it took a long time. No prisoner was ever absent without permission. In my term in the penal camps, I can't remember anyone attempting to escape. There were always guards with dogs inside the walls. Sentries along the perimeter carried rifles and had machine guns. But these precautions were unnecessary. Karelia itself—its forests and climate—was the most certain deterrence. Our prison was as secure as Devil's Island. The forest was as forbidding as an ocean, no one could survive for long in either element.

Following roll call, we rode a little train through the forest to our workplace, and toiled all day. Until the war, I had never done hard manual labor in my life, but I had been hardened by my recent travails. The months I had spent as a construction worker in Lwów had prepared me to some degree for the task ahead. My first job was felling trees. To do this, we were divided into teams of two and given simple hand tools. First, we chopped a "V"-shaped incision into one side of the tree. Then we took a long, traverse saw with handles at both ends, and bored a straight cut through the other side, stopping a few centimeters from the apex of the "V." By driving steel spikes into the incision, and beating them with the back of the axe, we made the tree crash down in the direction we desired.[15]

The instructors informed us that the state expected each two-man team to fell at least eight medium-sized trees a day. To earn our *payók*, or full ration of bread and soup, we would have to meet this quota. If we cut down more trees, we would get more food. Marx had argued against slavery, saying that because slave-laborers had no incentive to work hard, their work would always be unprofitable.[16] By introducing the quota system, our captors probably believed they were being good Marxists. The problem was that the food we were being served consisted of little protein and few vitamins. It was barely enough to sustain us in our work. The higher output of energy needed to surpass the quota far outweighed the meager benefits of getting larger servings of the low-quality food. We had already been weakened by our exile and transport, and it wasn't long before we started suffering from vitamin deficiency.

After a while, we were given a new task, splitting the felled trees into *dranki*, or flat boards, to be used in construction. The finished *dranki*, all of the same prescribed length, were tied up into bundles. I no longer remember what the quota was for this chore, but it certainly took long and hard work to meet it. We rarely exceeded the expected norm. There was a Soviet people's proverb that applied in the camps, too: "They pretend to pay us and we pretend to work."

In the evenings, there was a second roll call. Then, we ate dinner, soup and bread, every night. There was no meat and few vegetables. We all daydreamed about the kasha and borscht that we received on some state holidays. Sunday was a day for rest, but we were somewhat busy cleaning our clothes and trying to keep tidy. This was difficult, since we usually substituted leaves for toilet paper, and few items were as precious as a piece of soap.

Our conversation was about the future and the past. We all believed that this was just a chapter in our lives. I was sure that I would return to Oświęcim soon and resume my studies. I pictured the reunion with my mother and grandmother. Moreover, there was Belusia—maybe she would be waiting, too. Never once did I think that my destiny was to remain in this dreary, freezing prison forever. As for the present, all we could do was speculate. We had almost no knowledge of world events. At night, we slept the sleep of exhausted men, weary in every bone and fiber.

This daily pattern continued through the winter of 1940–1941. On the very coldest days, we were allowed a respite. Not surprisingly, the Soviets had a stern view of what temperature qualified as being too cold for working. They only allowed us to stay inside if the thermometer dropped below –40 degrees Celsius.[17]

The guards were humane, or at least not inhuman—many of them were prisoners themselves. I never experienced, or heard of, any beatings or torture. Our warders had an overwhelming predominance of force on their side, and for our part we showed little signs of resistance. The only time we stood up for ourselves was on Yom Kippur. It was cold that day, but not cold enough to pardon us from work. The guards came to mobilize us, but some of the more religious Jews in the camp refused to go. There was some pushing and shoving, but the determined prisoners insisted, saying, "this is our holiest of holies." *We will not work today.* Religion was not tolerated in the Soviet Union, but instead of using their power to make us work, the guards relented and gave us our holiday.

Besides us Polish detainees, the other prisoners in our camp were there either for political or criminal offenses. The criminals, stronger and more brutal, lorded it over the rest of us. Even the prison officials usually handled them carefully, often granting them extra privileges. Once, out in the forests, we were accidentally allowed to encounter some zeks from a nearby camp. They told us that they had been convicted of the political offense of being Zionists. This encounter made me realize that there were probably dozens of other camps and brigades working in these forests, all guilty of a different kind of "crime" against the State. Each one was carefully quarantined from the rest, so that the contagion of anti-Soviet ideas could be prevented.

Despite the change in my situation, I remained essentially the same person. I had always been absentminded. Typically, the one time I landed in the *kartser*, or stockade, as a troublemaker, it was this trait that had put me there. One evening, I returned to the camp and was shocked to find that the gates were locked. I was late. I have no recollection of what I had been doing. Escape was the last thing on my mind. Most likely, I had just had one of my periodic episodes of abstraction. Some thought had struck me and I had lost all track of time. I spent the night in the isolation cell, and in the morning I was released. In retrospect, it wasn't such a bad experience—no doubt I'd spent the night thinking peacefully about everything and nothing, which was often my favorite pastime.

Of all the things that I had packed in Oświęcim on September 2, 1939, only one was truly valuable to me—my father's wristwatch. I had lost many things in my life, through circumstances or carelessness, but I had held on to that. I had worn it across Poland, and kept it through the hard times in Lwów, when I probably could have traded it reasonably well for necessities. But it was the only family heirloom I had, nearly the last thing that connected me to the life I'd led in normal times.

At Karelia, I had hidden it in an inside pocket of my jacket. When I slept, I stored it in a crevice in the wall near my pillow. But at some point, one of the criminal inmates must had caught a glimpse of my secret treasure. One morning, on the train to work, this man made a lunge for the watch. We wrestled for it. He tried to pry it from my hands, while I strained my muscles to keep it. He was stronger and would have had it off me, but just as I was about to lose my grip, a guard intervened. He pulled us apart and told me to jump off the car. I scampered off, stunned, and grateful.

Several months had gone by. My daily routine in the camp was rough, but I had grown accustomed to my new life. The anxiety I had felt in Lwów during my first days under Russian power had gone. Then, I had spent every day, every minute, expecting to get arrested and interrogated. In Karelia, that time seemed like the distant past. I was not comfortable, but I was as secure as the situation could allow. The last thing I expected was for the Soviet secret police to take an interest in me now. So, that's exactly what they did.

Party officials arrived in the camp and interviewed many of the inmates. Tadek and I were called. Their questions were pointed and hostile, relating to our arrival in Lwów. When and how did we come to be in the Ukraine? What personal documents did we have? Had we sought Soviet passports? Why not? I faced their barrage as best I could and answered their questions. But, if I hoped to get some explanations of my own, I was mistaken. This was the first and only time that my case was discussed with any authorities. They never told me the accusations I faced, or the resulting penalties. Nor did I ever learn about the consequences, if any, of that hearing. Afterward, though, I didn't feel so secure.

In the spring of 1941, all of the prisoners in the camp were loaded into cattle cars and transferred. As with everything that happened to us, there was no explanation for this sudden change. Our new camp was hundreds of miles further east, in the Archangelsk region, near a town named Plessetsk. Once we were there, our lives were much the same as they had been. We did the same work, lived in the same type of barracks, and ate the same insubstantial food.

Our strength started to go. Tadek and I had pellagra, resulting from a lack of protein and vitamins, and suffered bouts of dysentery. We had lost weight and our eyes were bloodshot. The new camp had a little hospital. At first, we went there for a few short visits of a day or two. Then, we were admitted for a stay of several weeks. Dr. Schumacher, himself a long-term inmate, was in charge and often succeeded like a miracle-worker, despite the lack of needed drugs and even of needed food.

In hospital, we slept on real beds and dozed through roll call. The kind nurses were the only women we had seen in months. A gramophone was perhaps the most effective piece of equipment in the facility. The aria, "Una voce poco fa," from Rossini's *Barber of Seville*, sung by a Russian diva, was played repeatedly. It had been a long time since I had listened to classical music, and the sound was a medicine to me. Moreover, while we recovered, we finally began to hear some news from outside the camps.

The whole world was fighting. France had fallen, and only England still stood in the west. The United States remained neutral. Finland, having come under a Soviet attack and narrowly lost the "Winter War" of November 1939–March 1940, allowed the transit of German troops. Karelia was close to the fighting, and that was why all of us prisoners had been transported. In Plessetsk, we were hundreds of miles farther away from the front.

In June 1941, we learned that Hitler had broken his pact with Stalin, and the Nazis had invaded Russia. *Pravda* and *Izvestia* printed glowing reports of Red Army valor, and finally started describing German atrocities. The state newspapers claimed victory after victory, but each battle had been fought deeper inside the Soviet Union. Just like when I had faced it in 1939, the blitzkrieg appeared unstoppable.

The Soviets surrendered all their Polish acquisitions, leaving the Jews who remained in Lwów to fall into Nazi hands. Both sides destroyed crops and supplies, torching villages, scorching the earth. The Germans were eager to reach Moscow before the first frost, and the Russian generals wanted to stall for the arrival of their bitter ally, "Napoleon weather."[18]

In the infirmary at our camp near Plessetsk, we, of course, rooted for the Russians, simply because we knew that as bad as our treatment at their hands had been, it was better than what the Nazis would give us. At the time, it was difficult to see how the titanic struggle would affect our lives. But, it did. Suddenly international relations had changed. The Soviets and Nazis had become enemies, meaning that the Soviets and Poles were allies once again. In London, the Polish government-in-exile negotiated an agreement with the USSR. News reached us in our hospital beds—Polish prisoners of war were to be freed. They were even forming a Polish army. We could join our countrymen and get some long-awaited revenge.

Fantastic vistas opened up before us. We were free, we were in uniform reconquering Poland, and we were back in Oświęcim with our family. For years, we had been tossed around by one great force and then another. Finally, we had the power and volition to make decisions and take an active role in world events. Except, we couldn't even get out of our hospital cots. We were emaciated and weak beyond description. By the start of 1942, under Dr. Schumacher's care, I was starting to recover. But Tadek remained bedridden and feeble, terrible to see.

By late January 1942, my strength had returned, and I felt ready to travel. Tadek showed no sign of progress. I got increasingly frustrated and concerned. As Soviet methods and policies varied, I felt this amnesty offer could be rescinded at any moment. This might be my only chance to get out of the camp. I discussed it with the doctor and he gave me permission to leave. Then, I talked to Tadek. I didn't feel right leaving him. He had been my only friend and support through all our troubles. We had come so far together. But, just like my mother and grandmother had done that day in Zator, Tadek made the decision for me. He insisted that I leave him. I should go and save myself, while I could. When he recovered, we agreed, he would join me.

So, I left him in the hospital and walked out of the camp where I had stayed for a little more than a year and a half. It was the middle of winter and the railroad station was miles away. After a day's hike I made it with desperate effort to another camp and stayed the night. I showed my papers, which described my status and gave me permission to travel to a place called Novo-Sukhotino in Northern Kazakhstan. I had managed to save some food, but my attention must have wandered, and my crust of bread was stolen upon my arrival at the strange camp. Stealing from fellow inmates was considered a serious crime, but I knew no one here and didn't report it.

The next day, I finally arrived at the Plessetsk station, very weak and tired. I paid for my seat with some money they had given me, and boarded a train running south on the Archangelsk–Moscow line. My ticket got me to Vologda, a major rail depot more than halfway to the capital. The station was crowded, and the lines were choked with supplies headed toward besieged Leningrad and other crucial sectors of the front.[19] I wasn't feeling well, but I managed to find a seat on a train going east toward Sverdlovsk.

This was another slow and painful journey. The passenger cars were packed with people. It took energy and cunning to find places to sit and sleep. I was feeling ill, perhaps I hadn't been as ready for the tough trip as I'd thought. The lingering effects of my imprisonment were oppressive. I was dizzy and disoriented, but worst of all I felt very lonely. When I had arrived in Lwów after the war, I had been with my brother. Nearly three years later, in the middle of a vast, strange nation, I was totally alone.

We pulled into the Molotov station, deep in the Russian Urals east of Moscow. This was the end of the line. I was supposed to switch to another train on the Trans-Siberian Railway for the last leg of my journey south and east into Kazakhstan. I felt weak. The crowds pressed in on me. I fainted. When I woke, I was in a large metropolitan hospital, and I had no idea how I had gotten there.

Love in Ili

5 ■ ■ ■ By January 1942, the citizens of Leningrad were down to a quarter-pound of bread apiece per day. Since the previous September, when the *Blokada*, or siege, had begun, ration-levels had been cut five times. Now, in an ungodly winter, the pittance of food was no longer enough to sustain human life. In the next two months, 200,000 in the city would starve to death.

To ease the supply situation, the Soviet authorities ordered the evacuation of one-quarter of the remaining population. Half a million people would have to leave, and there was only one way out—an exposed road hacked through the ice of Europe's largest lake—the 125-mile-long Lake Ladoga. They rode unheated trains from Finland Station in the city, to the water's edge. There, they were transferred onto buses or open trucks for the desperate sprint across the ice. If all went well, the trip only took a couple of hours. But the wrecked vehicles that crouched along the road were the evidence that the journey rarely went well. Nazi planes and artillery attacked at all hours. The evacuees, already weak from their starvation diet, died by the thousands. Despite the dangers, this was the route to salvation, and the Russians called it the "Road of Life."[1]

This titanic struggle was reaching its climax in the frozen North, where darkness falls by 3:00 P.M., and temperatures routinely reach fifty degrees below zero.[2] I knew these conditions well from my time in Karelia and Plessetsk, but thankfully I had been placed sufficiently further east of the

German front. Like so many others in late January 1942, I lay close to death because of malnutrition. After collapsing on the train from Vologda, I had opened my eyes in a hospital in Molotov, with no memory of the ambulance journey.

It was a telling comment on my state of mind that one of my first emotions was anxiety. The Soviets had given me permission to travel to Novo Sukhotino in Kazakhstan, and that was all they had allowed me to do. By getting sick and passing out, I had violated the orders in my papers. However, I was too sick to fret for long.

For several weeks thereafter, I was in a state of profound torpor or coma. When conscious, I was attended by nurses who in my fancy were like angels of mercy, superior in charity, kindness, and efficiency. The doctors worked diligently, but they were handicapped by an almost complete lack of medicines. The best cure was food. I devoured everything that was offered. I was famished when I fell asleep, and starving when my hunger woke me a few hours later. Between meals, I felt the same longing for food, the anxiety about my next meal, which I had developed during my time at the camps. This feeling would stay with me for a long time.

Once, we were given a small orange as a special treat for supper. I was too excited to eat it at once. To prolong the pleasure, I carefully secured it under my pillow and finished it slowly the next day.

My surroundings had a short present and a long past. Molotov had only been Molotov for a few years. Until 1940, the city had been known as Perm. In the Ural mountains, almost 1,000 miles east of Moscow, it had always been a key rail juncture and industrial center. Since the start of the war, the population had swelled with the arrival of refugees from the conquered border areas. All industrial plants had been given over to the military, and Soviet tanks rolled off the lines twenty-four hours a day.

The front was far away, but from my hospital bed I could plainly see some consequences of the war. Every cot in my ward was occupied by students from a technical school who had escaped Leningrad across the perilous "Road of Life." They had been too young to fight, and now they were too sick to do much of anything. I was just over twenty-two-years-old and, like them, very skinny and weak. Their diets may have been even worse than my own, but they had not been forced to labor as I had to earn their rations. They were Russians indoctrinated in the Soviet system whereas I had been a foreign *zek* (an inmate of a Soviet labor camp), a Jew from Poland who had seen the Gulag first-hand. In the war between Hitler and Stalin, I rooted for Stalin, like all these young men. However, after the camps, I would never again feel sympathy for the Soviet cause.

My Russian improved through conversing with my fellow patients. They told me about the siege in Leningrad, where frozen bodies were piled in the streets, wrapped in blankets and resting on children's sleds. We didn't talk politics. They weren't up to it and I also wasn't up to it. And even if I had been, I had long since learned to be discreet. Once again, I was struck by the strength and kindness of the Russian people. So far, with the exception of the criminal who had tried to steal my watch, I had liked all the Russians I met. It was easy to separate my regards for the citizens from my hatred for their regime. But, in the hospital, I didn't make friends. The students from Leningrad dropped like flies, and no hospital bed remained empty for long. New patients were immediately brought in to replace the dead. As I started recovering, I worried that soon I would no longer qualify for a hospital bed. Clearly, there were others in more desperate need.

The doctors and nurses there saved my life. My desire to leave the camps had carried me through an arduous journey, but by the time I had reached Molotov, I had used up all my reserves of strength. I had had no conception of how sick I had been until I started to recover. I thought of Tadek's likely fate. He had been even sicker than me. In the camp clinic he would have received far worse care than I had been lucky to get in Molotov. Still, I hoped more with my heart than head that he had regained his health. Perhaps he would be waiting for me in Kazakhstan. Sometime in late April 1942, the doctors told me that I would have to relinquish my bed. They gave me new papers for my journey to Novo–Sukhotino, and even made sure that I got a ride to the train station.

After a three-month break, I again had to fight my way to get on board the train, this time the Trans-Siberian Railway. As usual, it was everyone for themselves, in very difficult circumstances. Typically, the Soviet authorities ordered people to go here or there, but made no attempt to help them do it. Everyone was expected to obey, despite the fact that it often was almost impossible to do so.

The situation resembled broadly the crush on the roads of Poland in 1939, but there everyone had fled on his own and there was no command or supervision. Neither situation worked very well. Both systems were under tremendous stress. So many people wanted to go in one direction — away from the Nazis. The trains were full of passengers on top and hanging on the doors. And nothing of that was new, but instead had probably been the same in any of the previous wars.

The enormous steam locomotive spit smoke and carried me across the desolate Urals. At Sverdlovsk, I was to switch trains and I had a few hours to myself in the city. In 1918, when it was still known as Ekaterinburg, this was where the Bolsheviks had assassinated Nicholas II and his family. Now, thanks to a recent five-year plan, it was an industrial center that turned out much of the country's arms and ammunition. At 1,600 miles east of Moscow, Sverdlovsk was safe from a German attack. It was a fine day and I enjoyed my first chance to see a large Russian city. Here, there was little sense of a war going on. Perhaps there were fewer young men around than usual, but it wasn't obviously the case. The Soviet people were working hard and their morale seemed high. I went to a movie and saw a beautiful film adapted from the famous novel by Lermontov, *Gheróy Nashego Vremeni*, or *A Hero of Our Time*. It was the first film I had seen in several years.

The next leg of my journey took me southeast, another thousand miles or so, to Petropavlovsk, in Kazakhstan. I had left the Arctic world of the camp in Plessetsk in January. Having traveled thousands of miles by rail, I arrived at the blazing height of summer. It was just a short distance to my final destination, the small settlement of Novo–Sukhotino. This was where my pass had directed me all this time, an isolated hamlet on the barren steppes in the far reaches of the Soviet empire.

I didn't know it at the time, but I was part of a large reshuffling of Polish deportees from the camps in the northwest to the provinces in the southeast. Centers were established in Uzbekistan, Kirghizistan, Turkmenistan, and Tadzikistan, but Kazakhstan was the main congregation point. A few years before I arrived, American travelers had described the enormity of this nation:

So large is Kazakhstan that it seems to stretch interminably from beyond the Volga to the copper mountains of the Altai near China, and from the Trans-Siberian Railway south to the towering snow-capped peaks of the Tian Shan. A map of its 1,059,800 square miles placed on a map of the United States would cover all the states as far south as North Carolina and as far west as the Rockies.[3]

Now this huge area was filling up with people from the westernmost reaches of the Soviet Union, mainly Poland.[4] We were far from the front and there was plenty of labor for us to perform. Rich in oil and coal, zinc, iron, lead, and tin, Kazakhstan had become an arsenal for the Soviet Union in the war.[5]

The hardships I had faced in Karelia and Plessetsk—were not extraordinary, but typical for the Gulag, and many other Poles in Kazakhstan had been through the same ordeal. We met, lived, and worked together. Not surprisingly, there was much awareness among us of how much we shared: common language, home country, wartime losses and camp experiences, and hopes of survival and return. Yet, some animosity to Jews carried into exile.

The Catholics had converted an old building into a church, which most of the community attended. I realized that I hadn't met any other Jews in this whole settlement of thousands of refugees. Though I was received well as a fellow Pole, at times I felt uncomfortable about the unusual imbalance.

One and a half million Poles had been deported from the Soviet-occupied area during the first half of 1940. One third of these were Jewish.[6] Like me, they had faced the arduous train journeys into the heart of Russia. The women and children, and some of the men, had been taken to remote areas, such as Kazakhstan, and left on their own. Most of the strong young men had gone through years of imprisonment and hard labor in the Gulag penal camps. Karelia had been bad, but there were worse places. The zeks, who mined gold in the camps at Kolyma, had died at an unbelievable rate. All of these Poles and Jews had one thing in common, the Soviets considered all of them to be enemy nationals.

That changed when the Germans invaded in June 1941. The Polish exile-government in England signed a pact with the Soviet Union, and we became allies. This is what led to my release from Plessetsk; around the USSR the other deportees were also being freed and directed toward settlements like Novo–Sukhotino.[7] Once we were free we needed to be fed, and a large international effort was made to send food and supplies to the Polish refugees in our scattered towns and villages. In these communities, the old relationships returned from before the war. In my case, we were more aware of the ties that made us close than of the traits that made us different. In general, that seemed to be the case in other places, too. Many Jews were put in positions of authority in the relief effort and took a hand in distributing supplies.

But there were exceptions. In a settlement in the Kirghiz Republic, Jews were threatened and taunted by the Polish relief distributors. "It even reaches the point that Jews—though they may qualify for and be entitled to it—are not put on the list of Polish citizens," wrote a visiting doctor, "and statements such as 'You will never see Poland again' or 'You are not needed in Poland' are a common occurrence."[8] The Jewish Press Service reported, "Jewish groups are claiming that the Polish Relief Committee, which was created to provide relief supposedly to all Poles, is not allocating this relief fairly to Polish Jews, since certain *Endek* (National Democrats— right-wing Anti-Semitic party) elements hold sway on the Committee."[9] The Endeks again. These were the National Democrats, the same fascist bullies who had driven me from classes in Kraków.

I didn't see this. Most people were friendly, and I don't remember anyone as hostile. Perhaps it was because I was one of the few Jews around and posed no threat, or maybe it was due to the fact that I kept to myself as much as possible. I was cautious and I certainly didn't hide, but also certainly didn't flaunt being Jewish. I knew by then that I was not regarded as a legitimate Pole. At this point I felt far more solidarity with other zeks, who had gone through the ordeal of the Gulag, than with people who just happened to have been born in the same country as me.

We eagerly followed the news about the war. The Red Army halted the invasion of the Soviet Union at Leningrad and Moscow. The Germans pushed forward through most of the Ukraine, but their assault on Stalingrad on the Volga was being fiercely resisted. Close to us, general Władysław Anders organized a Polish army from former prisoners of war (he himself had been held in the dreaded Lubianka prison) and deportees. In 1942, under intense British and Polish pressure, that force was permitted to leave the Soviet Union for Iran and Iraq, to fight the Germans in the Mediterranean Theater. Some of the Novo–Sukhotino men managed to join the Anders army and leave, but many, like myself, were not well enough to do so.

In Novo–Sukhotino, I was in a sort of limbo. I didn't make friends, though I grew acquainted with the men who worked with me. We managed to make a little extra money by walking out onto the steppes and gathering dried cow feces, called *kizyaki*, which was used for fuel in this mostly treeless land. We all battled the extreme summer heat, which even the Soviets admitted was unbearable. "One may wander for a whole day on the superheated sand . . . without meeting a single living thing," wrote a Russian geographer. "There are neither birds nor animals. All around is deadly silence. One waits in vain to hear the song of birds, the chirping of crickets, the noise of leaves."[10]

I had a few Polish books to read at night, but there was no movie theater or other organized entertainment. I don't think it was a particularly pleasant place. And I have few memories of the months I spent there. Most of my energy was spent trying to get out.

Bulletins filled with family notices were published sporadically by the Polish-deportee communities. Thousands of husbands, wives, parents, and children were desperate to get in touch with one another. I scanned the pages constantly, searching for any word from my relations. Each issue brought disappointment, until finally I found a few lines from my aunts Fryda and Eda. They were living in Ili, near Alma-Ata, the capital of Kazakhstan, and were looking for Tadek and me. Just reading and rereading their notice was a pleasure and relief. For the first time in months, I could be sure that somewhere out there, some part of my family remained alive.

It was not difficult to get permission to join them. It would mean another long journey to the east—my aunts had gone about as far as they could go, right to the border with China—but traveling had become almost a routine for me. I planned out the best route. Then, on the eve of my journey, I discovered that my papers were missing. These were the documents issued to me in the camp at Plessetsk. In the Soviet Union, no piece of property could be more important. Without my ID, I would not be able to travel at all. The guards would stop me before I had stepped foot on the train.

I don't know whether I had misplaced the papers in one of my frequent moments of absent-mindedness, or if someone in the settlement had stolen them from me. At first, it seemed as if I had been thwarted from reuniting with my family. After all my suffering and wandering, I felt as if I had reached the final door only to find it locked. But, I refused to give up and took decisive, possibly reckless, action. In the Molotov hospital I had started gathering pieces of soap. Ever since then, I had continued to expand my collection. The ruble was so shaky that barter was common, even preferred. Everyone learned to barter, and I had grown adept at it. Soap was a rare and valuable commodity and I could exchange it for anything I needed: whether it was a piece of cheese, or a new set of identification (ID) papers.

Therefore, I stepped onto the train at Novo–Sukhotino as Mikhail Vassilievich Dyatłovitski. The ID had no photograph and Mikhail shared roughly my own age and physical description. Traveling with a false passport was a grave offense, and I quailed at the thought of the repercussions. My only hope was that in the general chaos of the war, my lone transgression would go unnoticed.

My route took me first some 200 miles straight east across Siberia to Omsk, a large city where I had to change trains. I remember walking along streets made of wooden planks, which covered a massive morass of mud. I had no problems on this leg of my trip. Anyone who looked at my papers just gave them a glance and waved me by. From Omsk, I headed south on the Turkestan-Siberia Railway to Ili, a distance of about 800 miles. Known as the Turksib, this railroad had been built in 1926, by none other than my neighbor's notorious relative, Feliks Dzierżyński.[11]

On this train, I got a real scare. The militia took all of the passengers' documents and put them through a close inspection. At a stop in a remote town, the soldiers started calling names, mine among them. We were led off the train and into a police station. The locomotive steamed off without us. Night was falling. I was certain that my crime had been discovered, but I knew that my only chance was to remain calm.

A low-level apparatchik, obviously frustrated by his remote posting, examined my papers and leveled a suspicious glance at me. Having memorized the information on my card, I answered his questions confidently. I was Mikhail Dyatłovitski. After a tense moment, I was dismissed. I spent the night at the station, and the next morning I was put on a new train. It was with indescribable relief that I watched that station—and its bored bureaucrat—vanish in the distance.

From Alma-Ata I took a commuter train north to the town of Ili. It was the end of summer 1942. I had been traveling since January, but finally I had arrived. I found the address and entered. Suddenly, I was with family again. I got a warm greeting from my aunt Fryda and her husband Józef Stock, as well as aunt Eda and her daughter, Janka. They were shocked by my emaciated appearance. I still bore the marks of starvation that I had earned in the camps, even though I had been out of Plessetsk for more than six months.

My relatives had had their own share of difficulties. The families of my three aunts had fled to Lẃow in September 1939, where Wilek and Szymek had some property. On the way, they stopped in Łańcut and hid some jewelry in a garden near our former house, but it was never recovered. Eda and Fryda, with their husbands and Janka, were deported to Siberia in 1940, to a village called Afino near Tomsk in the district (oblast) of Novosibirsk. Szymek died there of a heart attack on December 7, 1942.

Eda and Janka, Fryda and Józef Stock were allowed to leave for a warmer climate and departed by train to Ili in Kazakhstan. Wilek, however, because of his illness, was never deported and his family found itself in 1941 under the Nazis. We were later told that he was mistreated and also died of a heart attack. They tried to save Jerzyk by getting a peasant's family to let him live with them and conceal his identity as a Jew, but he was betrayed. Paula did not survive either.

In Ili, Stock worked as an intermediary between the Polish refugees and the Soviet officials. When I told him about my adventures, he insisted that we destroy the false set of papers that had gotten me to Ili. We burned them immediately, and he helped me get a new passport in my own name. He also found me some new clothes, as mine had suffered during my trip.

We exchanged news, none of it happy. I told them about leaving Tadek, and we agreed to immediately place notices for him in all of the refugee newsletters. They told me that they had received no word from my mother or grandmother. I gave them news about their sister, Paula. On that day in Lwów when I had been locked inside the cattle car waiting for deportation, she had walked along the rails calling out my name. I had waved to her and she had seemed to cry. No one had heard from her since.

My aunt Eda allowed me to stay in the apartment with her and her daughter, Janka, whom I had last seen as a child in Katowice. It was modern and pleasant. For a single family it would have been quite comfortable, but I had to share a bedroom, and the conditions became somewhat cramped. Still, compared to what I had been used to, it was an enormous improvement. From the horror of the camps, and the anonymity of my wanderings, Ili represented a haven and a home. The Soviets were friendly and finding my next meal was no longer a matter that required cunning and forethought. It was all new, easier, and better. I was with people who really knew me and had been genuinely happy to see me. For the first time since the war began, I had a sense of being home.

Ili, I soon gathered, was a small town on the large river Ili, which flows from western Sinkiang, a province of China, into Lake Balkhash, a feature of southeastern Kazakhstan. The temperature climbed well above 100 degrees and the steppes exploded with the color of sunflowers and a brilliant red flower known as the *karandik*.[12] The refugee settlement here was large and well established. Heavily Polish and Jewish, its population rivaled that of the village, which consisted mainly of Russians and some Kazakhs engaged in farming, industry, and trade. The two different populations intermingled; some refugees lived together with the locals in their cottages.

Janka was a happy teenager, five years younger than me. She had grown surprisingly in the three years since I had last seen her. Like young people will, she was adapting to her new life and was even attending a school, which had been established—with Soviet consent—by the Jewish refugees. One teacher in particular had organized the entire operation. Her name was Lena Engelman, a Jewish refugee from Warsaw. I thought she was very pretty.

Lena (short for Leonarda) came from a religious and wealthy family. The Engelmans were among the more prominent Jewish families in the nation, as one of her forefathers had fought on the Polish side in an uprising against the Czars, and a street in Pułtusk—Ulitsa Engelmana—was named in his honor. The family had real estate holdings in the city, but also held land in the country and owned a working farm, which was almost unheard-of for Jews in Poland. Lena's father had been opposed to his daughter's going for higher education, but she had insisted, and moved in with an aunt in Warsaw.

In 1939, she had fled alone to the Russian side and was deported from there all the way to Tashkent, the capital of Soviet Uzbekistan. There she met with some activist refugees who had contacts with people in Ili and helped her to get here. By herself, she had made the same journey that I had taken—an impressive accomplishment for a woman traveling alone. Her Russian was excellent and she was a natural organizer. She was amazingly determined and ready to do any work to support herself and survive. Thus, even initially in Ili, she joined the men in collecting *kizyaki* in the steppe.

When I met her, she was deeply committed to the orphanage and school. It was the most important work of her life, and she was relentless in raising support by petitioning the Soviet and the London Polish authorities. In my entire wartime experience I had noticed again and again how people seemed to focus on their needs in times of emergency. Yet, Lena was devoting herself to the greater good.

We talked and flirted. She impressed me and seemed impressed with me. I was poor like a mouse; my only possessions were the clothes on my back and the lumps of soap that I had been able to scrounge together. But under circumstances, this was not surprising and not important. What really mattered and moved us were the many similar experiences we had shared. Both of us had been students at Polish universities. At Warsaw University, where Lena had studied history, she had also faced harassment by the Endeks. We both had relatives trapped in Nazi lands. And, we were both starved for love and affection. The war had interrupted our lives at a crucial moment, and neither of us had had much experience, or opportunity, for romance. Even in Ili, it was almost impossible to find an intimate moment alone. Neither of us had an apartment or even a bedroom. Lena lived in a primitive cottage with a Russian woman from Leningrad. It had a garden in the back, and it was there on a warm night that we first made love.

My family did not approve. They said Lena was too old for me, though she was just one year older than I was. My aunts had already picked out another woman for me to marry, but I wasn't interested. There was also some antagonism between Lena and Józef Stock. She often complained that her school received little help from his group of would-be administrators of the settlement. She went directly to the Soviets and established herself as a rival for their patronage. For me, choosing sides was not difficult. I took Lena's side. Soon, she moved to a different cottage closer to the school. I moved in with her. In normal times, this might have caused a scandal. But in Ili, where the living quarters were so cramped, even my aunts agreed it was for the best.

I got a job teaching at a school. I had tutored in Oświęcim, and this wasn't so different. My subjects were history and Polish literature and language. We made friends with the school's director, Pani Flankowa, the teachers Edward Koffler and his wife Anna, as well as the well-known Polish poet and writer Aleksander Watt (a pseudonym for Chvat) and his wife. We had good students, and for me it was satisfying to be back in an academic setting. It had been years since I was able to devote myself to any kind of studying at all. Our time was our own. In the evenings, we listened to the radio. We also had a phonograph with some modern records, and Lena and her girlfriends taught me to foxtrot. I had never danced before in my life. Lena and I agreed to marry, but we decided to wait until the war was over. In short, it was a happy period, an almost idyllic interlude. In the midst of war, in a faraway place, I had found love and joy. And I was continually amazed at my good fortune.

Alma-Ata, a provincial capital dwarfed by the snowcapped mountains that rose behind it, was only an hour's train ride away. The city whose name means "Father of Apples" in Kazakh language, had indeed large avenues lined with great shade trees watered by flowing rivulets that ran along the roads. There are several fine parks and orchards, and an impressive view to the north of the tall Alatau mountain range. In springtime, when the apples were blooming, it was especially beautiful. "The countryside," a traveler noted, "was a veritable paradise of gardens. The fragrance of apple, plum, and cherry blossoms filled the railway carriage with an indescribably delightful aroma—so very welcome after the dust of the desert."[13]

The city boasted an old wooden Russian Orthodox cathedral and a good-looking modern opera house. Lena and I once took our children for an afternoon ballet performance of folk dances from various Soviet republics. On another occasion, we went there alone in the evening and attended a well-done grand opera, Verdi's *Otello*. It was a rare feast for us, considering how, when, and where it happened.

Whole industries, and a great many workers, had been transplanted from the western republics and lands of the Soviet Union to the eastern regions, especially Kazakhstan. A huge amount of work, much of it defense-related, was being done around the new industrial centers far behind the front, among others near Alma-Ata. The commuter railroad from Ili was kept running several times each day and no special permission was needed to use it. This in itself was an unusual thing to see in the Soviet Union. Many of us took full advantage of it. I worked on various side jobs in Alma-Ata during school vacations, sometimes together with a good friend of mine,

Jacek (Yatzek) Halpern (in Russian, Galpern). As I remember, we guarded large heaps of cotton wool and cotton batting.

The sights and sounds in the countryside were more mixed than those in the city, and the national and local themes were more prevalent. In the evening, people walked around singing popular folk songs, called *chastooshki*, some of them very melodious and captivating. Young recruits marched, singing military and patriotic tunes, in the old Russian manner, a soloist ("zapyevayła") intoned a song, and a chorus of voices responded. Caravans of camels trotted in the desert, donkeys brayed, muezzins called for prayer from minarets, but the latter seemed rare, and Lena recalled seeing many more of them in Uzbekistan.

I got seriously ill twice, first with typhoid and then with jaundice. In each case, it required weeks of hospitalization for me to recover, but I got good care and enjoyed frequent visits from Lena, my family, and friends. Over time my health did, after all, improve and strengthen. I put on weight and, physically at least, put my time in the Gulag behind me.

I became still more forgetful and often heedless, suffering casual losses and thefts, sometimes under funny circumstances. Once, after I swam in the river Ili and sunned myself on its bank, I could not find my pants, which someone may have taken—and came back in my underwear. Another time, I was supposed to sell a sack of wheat to earn some money for the family. On the train ride to the mountains I was reading a Russian edition of Tolstoy's *War and Peace*. I became completely engrossed in my reading, and when I finally looked around my wheat had been stolen from there.

The military news had finally turned positive. The pivotal event was the capitulation of the encircled German forces at Stalingrad. There followed a sequence of powerful Red Army counteroffensives. In January 1940, the Russians were back at the prewar Polish border. Once again, as in September 1939, the names of Polish cities appeared in newspaper coverage of the fighting. But this time, the front was moving west.

In April, the Red Army had retaken Tarnopol, in the Ukraine. In July, the Soviets entered Lwów. In January 1945, Warsaw, almost totally destroyed, was finally liberated. A week later, Kraków was in Russian hands. And a few days after that, the Red Army arrived in Oświęcim, my hometown that had fallen to the Nazis early in September 1939. What the Russian soldiers found there, and in the neighboring town of Birkenau, would still not be known for quite some time.

For the first time, we began to imagine the postwar world. In particular, we wondered about the future of Poland. We knew that there was an exile-government in London that had organized relief efforts for the deportees. But there was a real possibility that the USSR might succeed in turning Poland into a puppet state. This became more threatening when the Soviets started a strong campaign among us refugees in favor of a new organization called the Union of Polish Patriots or *Związek Patriotów Polskich* (ZPP in Polish abbreviation).

Meetings with compulsory general attendance proclaimed that all Poles must work to create a new, sovereign, and independent homeland at peace with its neighbors from south and east.

Prudence and the desire to return argued for compliance, and this fell easy since controversial issues such as the political complexion and the borders of the future nation of Poland were not brought up for the time being. I recall no official stand against the London regime and no serious political debates in any of the meetings. Rather, it is my recollection that people known for their political differences generally took the campaign for ZPP in stride, without either clear enthusiasm or clear opposition. Some, used to the Soviet propaganda, may have dismissed it as such too lightly. Those of us, who had seen the Gulag system, assumed that this manipulation would have sinister results in the future.

On April 30, 1945, Adolf Hilter committed suicide. A week later, the war was over. Of course, everyone in our far corner of the world rejoiced unconditionally at Germany's "unconditional surrender." We began eagerly expecting to return to Poland, but those hopes were soon dashed. Every passing week made us more anxious as we began to wonder if we would ever be allowed to leave the USSR. For months we heard absolutely nothing from the authorities.

There were enormous difficulties to be resolved. In typical Soviet style, the process was made far more complicated than it had to be. Living in Asia, we had the lowest priority of return. There were papers to be filled out and certificates to be obtained. These passes could only be issued by the ZPP, and after that every person had to be vetted by the NKVD (People's Commissariat of Internal Affairs), Stalin's secret police force.[14] Perhaps even more than the practical problems, there were diplomatic issues at stake. At the Yalta Conference in February 1945, England and the United States had yielded to Russian insistence on turning postwar

Poland into a Soviet satellite. The USSR would keep all the territory it had occupied in September 1939. The new government of Poland would be of Stalin's choice.

None of this struggle was reported in the local newspapers in Kazakhstan, but we could imagine the vague outlines of the issue. It was clear, even then, that the precarious alliance between east and west would not long outlive the war.

We heard vague reports that some returning soldiers who had been captured and held in Germany were being deported to forced labor camps. All contacts with the west had become suspect again. Even if we were to return to Poland, it would not be the free Poland of our youth, but a protectorate under Soviet influence. Nevertheless, we still wanted desperately to go, and late in the year rumors arose of our likely repatriation next spring. Despite all uncertainties, the time had come to prepare for a new life together, hoping going back in what to us was still "the West."

On January 12, 1946, a Saturday, Lena and I went to a civil registrar's office in Ili and were married in the brief, official Soviet ceremony. That evening, my family decorated their apartment and laid out what was then a sumptuous feast for the reception. Any disapproval or constraint had long since vanished. We celebrated our wedding, and in a larger sense, we were rejoicing our good fortune. Within a few weeks, it was clear that Lena was pregnant.

In May 1946, a year after Germany surrendered, we, and the students and orphans from our school, boarded trains in Ili and began the long, long journey home. Compared with our 1940 trips to the Soviet camps and villages, the conditions were almost luxurious. Lena and I rode in passenger cars, while our students rode in freight cars that had been equipped with bunks. There was no food service, but we had been warned in advance, and allowed to pack our own provisions.[15]

Our route took us through Alma-Ata to Tashkent (west and slightly south), then to Kzyl-Orda near the Aral sea, Uralsk, and Saratov, where we crossed the Volga (going northwest). We crossed the Don at Voronezh, an area of fierce fighting during the war and a great Red Army attack at Kursk, finally through Gomel, Pinsk, and Brest to Warsaw, all northwest then west, altogether a distance of approximately 3,000 miles. I remember only a few scattered vignettes from the long trip: a salty plain and salt dealers around Kzyl-Orda; the long bridge at Saratov; vast steppes giving way to tall forests over long stretches of the journey; large cemeteries, a legacy of the war in the European part of the Soviet Union; and boiling water, or *kipyatók*, for tea, a fixture of most railroad stations in this huge country.

I don't remember exactly where we crossed the border into Poland in late May or early June 1946. I know the final destination of our train was Gostynin, a small town west of Warsaw, where we left the children from the Ili orphanage. Then, Lena and I faced the future. I had been in the Soviet Union for six years. During that time I had grown from a teenager who had led a quiet, studious life, into an adult, tested through adversities that a later generation could never understand. I was twenty-six years old, a married man with a family incipient. I had gained a lot, and had lost a lot. I keenly felt the disruption of my studies and career.

I had many visions, but few plans, for my future. I had been a world away from my former life, and, returning to Poland, I had little idea of what I'd find. What I didn't expect, what none of us expected, was that there would be nobody, absolutely nobody, left to greet us.

From the Ashes

6 ■ ■ ■ History records what had happened in Poland since I had seen it last. The number "six million" needs no explanation. The word "Holocaust" has a specific as well as a general definition. But in 1946, that was all still generally unknown and yet to come.

The Soviets had not prepared us for what we'd find. While the major state newspapers, *Pravda* and *Izvestia,* had been filled with stories about the war, I don't remember reading anything concerning the tragedies in Poland. In our local paper, *Kazakhstanskaya Pravda,* there were lurid reports of German atrocities at Leningrad and in the Ukraine; but about the annihilation of the Jews—nothing. I would have to learn the truth myself.

Lena and I made sure our charges—the young orphans from the Ili school—were in good hands. In that, we had the help of Rabbi Kahane of the Polish army. We then began to examine our own situation. Poland was not the nation we had known. We planned to take up our lives again, but really didn't know how to do it, or whether it would even be possible.

We arrived in the north, at Gostynin, a part of the country I had never seen. Warsaw, where Lena had gone to university, had been a major battlefront and a center of ghetto revolt, and was in ruins. Seventy-five miles to the southwest, Łódź, the nation's second-largest city, had survived the war unscathed. It became a *de facto* capital, along with Kraków, as well as a major gathering point for returning refugees. We headed there.

More than 200,000 Jews had lived in Łódź before the war; they had been ghettoized and then liquidated in Auschwitz and Chelmno. When the Red Army arrived in January 1945, there were about 900 Jews left alive. The fleeing Germans had left an abundant supply of available apartments, often with the furniture still in place. Refugees were directed here and, as they straggled in, the Jewish population began to grow again. Some came from concentration camps; others had hidden under false identities during the occupation, and many, like us, were returning from Russia. About 15,000 Jews were being housed in the city when Lena and I arrived in the summer of 1946.[1]

We were penniless. All of our worldly belongings could fit in a few suitcases. Aid societies had been established to distribute supplies. We received enough money to rent a tiny apartment of our own. The accommodations were simple and, we hoped, temporary. Our first priority was to reconnect with survivors from Lena's family. We registered at the Jewish committee with high hopes, which were soon dashed. Of her relatives, there was no news.

Being in Łódź could give a false impression of the fate of Poland's Jews. Besides the aid agencies and committees, there were prayer groups and Zionist organizations, literary evenings and theater performances.[2] The 15,000 Jews who now found themselves in Łódź were attempting to recreate the world they had lost, and at times it may have felt like they were succeeding. But these 15,000 were all that could be culled from all the neighborhoods of all the towns and cities of a nation. Tiny remnant though it was, the Łódź community represented one of the largest single assemblage of Jews anywhere in the country.

In 1939, there had been 3.5 million Polish Jews. Only 60,000 or so had survived in Poland. After the war, another 100,000 returned from the Soviet Union. Like me, they found themselves in cities far from their former homes. Some wanted to stay, most others were eager to leave for Palestine or the United States. There was constant motion, but in 1946, the Jewish population in Poland peaked at somewhere between 180,000 and 240,000 people—a minuscule remainder.[3]

When Jews had represented one-tenth of the total population, many Poles had resented their power and wealth. Now that the Jews had been through such torment that their numbers had become inconsequential, the Poles might have been expected to look at them with some compassion.

But, it was not to be. Those Poles inclined to anti-Semitism found new reasons for animosity, especially in the claim that Jews were conspiring with the Russians to install a pro-Communist government. Before, though large numbers of Jews had been poor, many Poles had insisted they were all rich. Now, though Jews represented the entire political spectrum, the Poles linked them all with the Soviets, and even coined a new word, *żydokomuna*, as shorthand referring to the perceived Jewish–Communist conspiracy.

There were attacks, isolated incidents here and there, resulting in some Jewish deaths. Tension and fear lingered and threatened to prevail. After the destructive fury of the war, we had hoped to find a better world. But it began to appear that no lessons had been learned. For concentration camp survivors, or for those of us who had made it out of the Gulag alive, this was particularly painful and disappointing.

Still, I didn't give in to hate. I believed that generalizing hate and responding to it in kind was wrong and futile. The Polish Catholics, like the Jews, faced a time of crisis. There was a general shortage of food and sporadic starvation. There was destruction and conflict everywhere. Looming above it all was the inescapable power of the Soviet Union. Poland was politically divided, almost in civil war. On the tail of victory was coming subjugation by another neighbor, but not independence. Poles were victims themselves, hence they would focus their frustrations on people that were even weaker and more victimized, which had always meant the Jews. As much so in 1946, as in 1936. Nothing had changed.

Once Lena, now very much pregnant, was settled in our apartment, it was time for me to return to revisit my old home in Oświęcim. The train ride was several hours long, and I had plenty of time to reminisce. I had seen too much to be hopeful about what I would find. Logically, I knew that the war had probably destroyed my old existence. It was clear that the odds of returning to my house and finding it unchanged, with my mother and grandmother alive and well, were very slim. But there was a chance, and I couldn't help but hope.

I stepped onto the platform of the station, which had been greatly expanded since I had last seen it.[4] Many more tracks had been constructed, so this had clearly become a busy railroad juncture during the war. I had no idea of what horrible purposes these new tracks had been required for.

Crossing the bridge over the River Soła, I came into the center of the town. Here was the fortress on the hill and the church—Oświęcim's post-card sights. There had been little fighting here, and most of the buildings were unscathed. However, the Great Synagogue was gone. The Nazis had torched it soon after my departure. I went to Belusia, my old girlfriend's house, but the family was gone. I walked the streets, looking for a familiar face, but found none. There were no Jews here.

Finally, I found someone I knew—a Polish family whose daughter had gone to school with me. Her parents told me that she had been killed, the victim of a stray bullet. They invited me to their home, and we sat together and wept. I plied them with questions. All the Jews were gone. My old violin teacher, a poor, gentle Pole, had been accused of anti-Nazi activities and was tortured to death. Then they described something that I had never imagined. The Nazis had built a death camp outside the town in Brzezinka (Birkenau in German). The expanded railroad station had been used to bring in victims, thousands everyday.

The stench from the chimneys had been sickening, they told me. All the people I talked to in Oświęcim that day mentioned the unforgettable smell of the smoke. When the Nazis had retreated, they had destroyed some of the chimneys at the camps. For miles around, the fields and earth had been covered in human ashes.

Leaving that mourning family, I went ahead in search of my own. I thought perhaps I could find some monument to my mother or grand-mother at the old Jewish cemetery near the River Soła. I had never vis-ited this place before the war. In a vibrant community, the dead had not seemed important, but now they were all that was left. Even here, I was disappointed. A bomb had detonated in the center of the grave-yard and several graves had been destroyed. Other stones had fallen over and many more, particularly the marble ones, had been stolen for use in construction—a common Nazi practice.[5]

It was a long walk across town from the cemetery to my old gymnasium. Above the entrance, the stone inscription about how "sweet" it is to die for one's country still remained, but now it merely reminded me of the millions who died in the just finished war in hatred rather than honor. In the office, I had the secretaries find a copy of my old diploma, the proof that I had passed my *matura* exams, which I would need if I was to continue my studies.

Then, I turned my steps toward home. I no longer believed that a miracle would occur, and that my family would be there waiting to greet me. But, there it was, the old house, exactly as I remembered it, except for a crack in one of the walls that must have been caused by Russian artillery. The garden was in bloom, and the fragrance and colors recalled countless memories. I knocked on the door.

A middle-aged Polish couple opened up. I told them who I was. They may well have been shocked to see me, and not at all happy, but they invited me inside. The furniture was different, but many of the appliances were the same as I remembered. I particularly noticed the wood stove in the living room that had kept us cozy on winter nights.

The mood was awkward and strangely impersonal. I had no idea who these people were. They didn't introduce themselves. They did not know whose house they had taken except that it had belonged to a departed Jewish family.

The couple had some American currency, which they offered me for the house. To drive down the price, they complained about the state of the structure, pointing to the crack in the wall as evidence. Their offer came to a few hundred dollars, a pittance in normal circumstances, but this was about the best I could expect in postwar Poland. Having seen Oświęcim, I knew that I had no intention of reclaiming my old possessions and resettling my family here. I accepted the money and left, to the relief of everyone involved.

It was time to go. I didn't attempt to see the camps. From the vague directions I had heard, I tried to figure out where they had been located. My impression was that they had to have been sited in the old barracks that had housed my aunt's textile workers before the war. Actually, I was wrong about this; it just showed how personal and immediate the death camps were for me. The whole world knows Auschwitz, but for those of us who had grown up there, the town still has an entirely different perspective as well. How could I, who associated Oświęcim with so many joys of youth, come to think of it as a place of tragedy? It would be years before I finally came to grips with this paradox.

I returned to the railroad station, and took the very familiar trip to Kraków. The damage done by the Luftwaffe in September 1939 had long since been repaired. Like Oświęcim and Łódź, this ancient city had survived the war with little damage. Except, of course, for Kazimierz, the

Jewish neighborhood, which was deserted. There had been 60,000 Jews in Kraków before the war; now 2,000 were left.

Classes had resumed at the university in February 1945. The dormitories, still dressed in the camouflage paint that had protected them from air raids, were crowded with students.[6] There had been few Jews enrolled here before the war, and there were almost none now.

The university had suffered under the Germans, who clamped down on all proud Polish institutions. In November 1939, the Nazi governor of the city had invited all the 160 members of the faculty to a "conference." When the guests arrived, they had found Gestapo agents surrounding the building. Most of the professors were deported to Germany, and the university was closed.[7] During the war, thirty-four professors and staff workers died in concentration camps.

My most famous professor had been Rafael Taubenschlag, an expert on ancient Greek and Roman law. He was Jewish, and the fascist Poles had ridiculed him and derisively called him, "Taubeles." It was from his class that I had been ejected during the "day without Jews," my most upsetting prewar experience of anti-Semitism. Taubenschlag had escaped to America in time to evade the Nazis. Like many prominent European intellectuals during the war, he taught in New York City at the New School for Social Research and Columbia University. He returned to Poland and taught in Warsaw, but committed suicide in 1958.[8]

I went to the registrar and got a certificate showing that I had completed two years of study. My business completed, it was time to return to Łódź.

My attempt to find out about my family had been a failure. I had learned nothing definite about my mother and grandmother. I knew they had been taken from Oświęcim to Będzin, a town some twenty kilometers to the north. I would never find out if they had been brought back to be killed in the concentration camps, so I concluded that they had probably died in the Będzin ghetto, along with many others. I would never know for sure what happened to them. Just as I could never find out exactly what had happened to my brother, Tadek.

However, the larger story was clear. And eventually, I would learn about the fates of the towns and cities I had known before the war.

In Łańcut, where I was born, the Jewish community had numbered about 3,000. I had last seen the town in September 1939, during my flight across the country. I was just a day or two ahead of the German invaders and had not had time to loiter. Three years after my visit, in August 1942, Nazis trucked the 5,000 Jews of Łańcut and the neighboring towns into the Palkinia Forests and slaughtered them.[9]

Count Potocki, the great nobleman of Łańcut, had fled with his mother to live under German protection in Vienna. When they abandoned their ancient castle, they took with them thirty truckloads of priceless art and treasures.[10] His fellow Poles denounced him as a collaborator, but many Jews continued to view him as a benefactor. The Nazis had planned to burn the beautiful seventeenth century synagogue, and had even piled up benches inside to prepare the blaze, but Potocki, it was said, had intervened to save it. The Great Synagogue was one of the few in Poland to survive the war intact.[11] But the Jewish community in Łańcut, which had been founded in the 1500s, was gone and would never be rebuilt.

Lwów, where I had stayed from late September 1939 until I was deported to Karelia, had had the third-largest population of Jews in the country. When I was there, the number of Jews had climbed up past 150,000, as refugees from the west fled the Germans. When we were taken to the Soviet Union, we had envied those who remained behind. But, in 1941, the Nazis seized the city and the Lwów ghetto became one of the most infamous of the war. In 1942, the Jews began to be sent to the death camp at Belzek. When the city was liberated in July 1944, only 800 Jews in Lwów were left alive.[12]

If Oświęcim was empty, and Kazimierz in Kraków was deserted, then Śofdmieście in Warsaw, and the communities in Łańcut and Lwów, and all the other Jewish neighborhoods in Poland had also vanished. It was a shock, and finally our disaster began to assume its true proportion. That whole world was gone.

Back in Łódź, Lena finally heard some good news. Refugees from Russia were still arriving. There were postings and newsletters. People registered and hoped to learn about their loved ones. Through these channels, we discovered that Lena's brother Sam, or Symek, had arrived in Warsaw. We immediately rushed there to greet him.

Sam had survived the war years in the labor camps of northwestern Russia, working mainly in the coalmines. Both Lena and he were overjoyed to find each other: the only surviving members of a large and close family. He seemed surprised at Lena's decision to marry without presence of, or consent from, anyone in her family. I may not have measured up to the great plans they had for her, at least initially. But he took the inevitable with good grace.

The coal mines that he had been in were the worst in the entire camps. Few were strong enough to make it through the war alive. Sam was short, but he was tough and very determined. Searching for others in the large family, he had one more success, discovering a young cousin named Dzidka, who had survived in hiding with the help of her old Polish nurse.

Finally, to reconnect with his past, Sam was eager to return to the Engelman family home. He visited the villa in Pułtusk and was greeted even more rudely than I had been in Oświęcim. His family had been rich and widely resented by the nearby Poles. When he arrived, he had also found squatters in possession of his estates. In my case the atmosphere had been awkward and a little tense. Sam sensed real danger, and decided to flee.

With no homes and very little money left, there was almost nothing but our memories to keep us here. Our debate what to do—stay and hope for a better future in a free Poland or give up such dreams right away and plan to leave as soon as possible—had now shifted more and more toward the latter. Sam argued for a determined effort to emigrate to America, and I agreed, having little hope for better circumstances now that the Soviets were so firmly in control. Lena, while not entirely persuaded, went along with us, understanding that there was little left for us here.

Then, a tragedy occurred that ended all debate. On July 4, 1946, in the nearby city of Kielce, a rumor circulated that fifteen gentile children had been kidnapped and ritually murdered by the local Jews. It was the kind of medieval lie that Jew-haters had been using for centuries to justify pogroms. Within hours, the Jews of Kielce found their community center surrounded. The police did nothing to prevent the inevitable violence, and about forty Jews, including women and children, were murdered by the mob.[13] That these victims had survived the years of Nazi rule only to fall to their own countrymen was the most heartbreaking part of the massacre.

The Communist government, which had failed to protect the victims, used the incident to call international attention to the anti-Semitism of the Poles and clamp down even harder on nationalist agitators. Justice was swift. Nine Poles were given show trials and then shot in the basement of their prison a little more than a week after the pogrom.[14] It was one of the few times in history that a Pole had been convicted of killing a Jew; and of course, it only increased the growing anti-Semitism, which was spreading rapidly.

The few remaining Jews now flooded toward the borders, desperate to escape the country. The exodus began immediately. In Warsaw, the Hotel Polonia, home of the American military attaché's office, was crammed with supplicants. Others looked to the Czechs, the British, and the French, hoping to somehow end up in Palestine. A few reportedly stowed away on ships, just to get away. By mid-August, the Polish government had granted less than 5,000 emigration permits, but it estimated that as many as 25,000 Jews had fled the country.[15]

Like most of the others, we were unable to get government approval to depart. But Sam took charge and made our plans. He learned of a train, sponsored by the American aid organization, HIAS (Hebrew Immigrant Aid Society), that would be leaving from Warsaw for the U.S. zone in Western Germany. The train was ostensibly intended to repatriate German Jews who had been sent to Poland during the war and now desired to return home. But no one seemed to be checking too closely, and we all registered for the passage.

We pulled out of the Warsaw station in September 1946. Dzidka, Lena's cousin, refused to accompany us and remained behind with her childhood Polish lover and nurse. Sam came along, and we both cared for Lena, whose pregnancy was now very advanced. Our possessions were few and easily portable. We had acquired almost nothing in our brief stay in Poland. Of most value to me were my certificates from gymnasium and university. I was growing increasingly impatient to renew my studies as quickly as possible and begin a career.

Before we had gone very far, it was clear that our train was not what it had claimed to be. That we were German expatriates had just been a cover story. Most, if not all, the passengers were Polish Jews eager to reach the west. To mask this fact, the organizers asked for volunteers who spoke German. I raised my hand, and was given a group to lead. In case anyone asked questions in German, we were supposed to answer, thus giving the impression that everyone in our group spoke the language like a native.

Lena had been nervous by my volunteering for this job, and my experiences in the war should have taught me to keep out of the spotlight. Indeed, when we reached the city of Stettin, on Poland's northwest border, it appeared that Lena's fears were about to be realized. Soldiers stopped the train and all of the volunteers were marched off into a local jail. This was the third time I had been pulled from a train. First, it had happened in Lwów, when I was separated from my brother. Then, I was detained on my way to Ili, when I had been using false papers. But this felt most dangerous to me. I had a wife and family now, and was in serious violation of the law. With freedom so close, it would have been unbearable to be stopped right at the border.

We spent the night in the jail, but were released the next morning. I believe that the soldiers were simply looking for a bribe, and someone must have paid them off. We quickly crossed into the Russian zone, and within a few hours, we had passed through a checkpoint in Lübeck and entered British-occupied lands. We headed southwest, through Hamburg and Bremen, both flattened out almost completely by bombing, then south for the rest of the journey, passing the British-occupied Rhineland to U.S.-occupied Hessen. After another long delay in Frankfurt am Main, we were through U.S. Controls, and all dangers were behind us.

We ended up in a displaced persons camp near the small town of Bensheim, about thirty miles south of Frankfurt. Run by the United Nations Relief and Rehabilitation Administration, these hastily set up camps housed more than 100,000 Jewish refugees in the U.S.-held areas of Germany. We shared an apartment near the old town. The lodging was cramped but the food was regularly delivered and adequate, which was the single most important factor at a time of great scarcity. While townspeople were selling valuables for food throughout the countryside, most of the refugees or "DPs" ("displaced persons") had nothing to sell and were literally saved by the food allotments.

Our camp housed more than 1,000 people from Poland and other parts of Eastern Europe. A thriving Jewish community, complete with synagogue and theater group, had been established. All of us had been in motion for years now. We had been uprooted so many times that we truly had become displaced persons in a literal and spiritual sense. It had been years and years since any of us had experienced the security of having a stable home. For Lena and I, creating that kind of environment for our family was a top priority.

Shortly after our arrival in Bensheim, I went with her to the German hospital in town. During the day, on Friday, October 4, 1946, our first son was born. He was a big, healthy baby. We named him Leopold (nicknamed Poldi) after my father, but since his early childhood he has been known as Steven.

He had been born just hours before the evening of Yom Kippur, the highest Jewish holiday. When I returned to the camp and announced the happy event at a meeting in the synagogue, the others rejoiced and told me it was an auspicious day to be born, which augured a great life for my son.

The Association of Jewish Students

7 ■ ■ ■ The disasters of 1939–1945—invasion, flight, war, partition, and defeat; threat of genocide and reality of deportation; loss of home, family, freedom, and everything but life—bordered on overwhelming. In the Gulag, so much concentration was required to survive from day to day, there had been little time to think about the future. In Ili, my energies were consumed with regaining strength and establishing an intimate relationship with Lena. Not before the end of the war could we start giving serious thought to how to get on with our lives and careers. And so, for us, 1946 opened with marriage in Ili and continued with the return to Poland and escape to West Germany. In September 1946, right after our arrival in the displaced persons camp at Bensheim, we decided to move to Heidelberg and resume our academic studies.

Our official residence was in the displaced persons camp in the small town of Bensheim, but the great educational center of Heidelberg, home to Germany's most famous university, was just a short train journey to the south. If I were to prepare for a future as an academically educated professional and an earning head of a family, Heidelberg was obviously the place to be. I didn't waste a day. Carrying the documents from Kraków University and the Oświęcim gymnasium, I looked into the possibility of enrolling in the fall term, which, providentially, was just about to begin.

During my first visit, I met the man who would become my closest friend. Marcel Tuchman, who had survived the ghetto in Przemysl,

Poland, and the concentration camp at Birkenau, was a medical student and a leader of the Jewish student community in Heidelberg. He told me right away of the opportunities that were available. The university was eager to distance itself from the Nazi past. The American authorities were interested in promoting the welfare of the survivors of the Nazi persecutions and Soviet deportations. My certificates from Poland would prove my academic standing and enrollment in the university law school would not be a problem. Best of all, the United Nations Relief and Rehabilitation Administration (UNRRA) would pay for my tuition.

It was a chance I couldn't pass up, even though it meant remaining in Europe for several more years, at a time when most Jews were using any available means to escape to America or Israel.

My son, Steven, had been born in Bensheim. Traditionally, the *bris*, or circumcision, takes place on the boy's eighth day. That this ceremony took place in Heidelberg, shows just how quickly and eagerly we transplanted ourselves to our new home. Steven's birth on the eve of Yom Kippur had been taken as a good omen. At the *briss* he urinated at the head of Marcel, who was holding him. I'm not sure what this signified, but it led to my son getting an affectionate nickname that translates roughly as "pissbaby." At the time, though, I was the only person in the room too nervous to laugh at the situation.

Heidelberg had been almost totally destroyed in the war—the Thirty Years War, from 1618–1648. During that religious combat it had been "five times bombarded, twice laid in ashes, thrice taken by assault and delivered over to pillage." The town, as a result of these calamities, had lost its medieval character and was dominated by baroque architecture dating from the seventeenth century.[1] Luckily, the latest war had not caused much damage. Red-roofed houses—mostly between two and four stories—were overpowered by great churches. Green in the summer, snowy in winter, nestled tightly between the mountains and the castle Schloss on one side and the River Neckar on the other, Heidelberg truly was a perfect German town, sprung from the pages of a fairy tale.

We found lodging in the home of a widow, Frau Professor Seitz, on Mittermeierstrasse, a narrow lane off the far busier Bahhofstrasse. The Frau Professor had a second-story apartment in a neat old house of white-painted brick, and we rented a bedroom from her. She was alone and there were three of us, so it was not hard to share the kitchen and bathroom. She helped us with childcare, and I'm sure she welcomed the company.

The university, a haphazard cluster of rather unimpressive buildings, had long been the center of the community. Like in Oxford or Cambridge, Heidelberg was defined by the institution in its midst. It was the most ancient university in Germany, although the Jagiellonian University in Kraków was actually a little older. Founded in 1386, at a time of widespread anti-Semitism, part of the college had originally been located in some confiscated Jewish houses.[2] It had originally trained Catholic priests, and after the sixteenth century, it had ordained Protestant ministers. By the twentieth century it had blossomed into a progressive center for science and philosophy.

When Hitler came to power, the school contained a high proportion of Jewish students and professors. However, by 1936, when the university celebrated its 550th anniversary with swastikas and storm troopers, the scene was very different. Nazis had taken down the inscription, "To the Living Spirit," which had stood over the gates, and replaced it with the words, "To the German Spirit." The sculpture of Athena was removed and a German eagle put in its place.[3] Jewish faculty members, or those with a liberal bent, were run out of the country, and racist gibberish was promoted to the level of "objective" science.

Philipp Lenard, professor emeritus at Heidelberg and winner of the Nobel Prize, was the Nazis' favorite physicist. "Research in natural science has never even been attempted by any people, except on the fertile soil of already existing achievements by Aryans," he wrote in the preface of his 1936 polemic, *German Physics,*

No Negro physics have ever been known; on the other hand, a peculiar physics of the Jews has been widely developed. . . . To characterize it briefly, one may perhaps best and most fairly point to the work of its most eminent representative, the full-blooded Jew, A. Einstein. His Theory of Relativity sought to transform and dominate the entire field of physics. Actually it is today completely played out. Indeed, it probably was never intended to be true; for the Jews are conspicuously lacking in any disposition toward truth.[4]

By the spring of 1945, when U.S. troops occupied Heidelberg, Hitler had done tremendous harm to the university's ancient reputation. The school, considered a hotbed of Nazism, was shut down for nine months.

American investigators dismissed 70 percent of the faculty for having Nazi ties, and kept a close watch on those who remained there. In January 1946, the rector, under the watchful eyes of American officers, declared that democracy was the key to Germany's future, and the university was officially reopened. Within a few months, 2,500 students were enrolled, which was about half of the prewar total. The United States gave the administration great freedom in restructuring the curriculum, but insisted—luckily for me—that 10 percent of the student body had to come from the masses of displaced persons.[5]

In 1946, many people were feeling very disillusioned with Europe. None of the fine philosophic and technological advances made on the continent since the times of the ancient Greeks had been able to prevent the rise of Hitler. It was tempting to believe that the Holocaust not only represented the end of European civilization, but also actually repudiated the centuries of European history. Like almost all Jews, I planned to leave. As soon as my studies were complete, I would emigrate to the United States or Israel. But I had lived my entire life in Europe, and of course I considered myself a European.

Heidelberg was as central to the history of Germany as Harvard was in America. Even the Nazis hadn't completely destroyed the attractions of the university for me. I knew that few academic institutions could rival it for historical importance. "Any attempt to give a catalogue of the names of celebrated men who have been more or less closely connected with Heidelberg must prove unsatisfactory," a nineteenth century visitor had written. "Everybody has been there."[6] Now, I would be there, too. And I felt that this was an honor as well as a privilege.

On a more practical plane, there's no way to explain how much more comfortable my daily life was in Heidelberg than it had been during the preceding years. Nevertheless, we were still in the nervous situation of being some of the last Jews left in Germany. Our scholarships made it possible for us to remain, but it was the Association of Jewish Students, which I joined immediately, that made it bearable, and even enjoyable.

We were the first Jewish student organization in Germany since the early years of Hitler's reign, and for celebratory and justifiable propaganda reasons, the United Nations and its democratic and liberal partners, notably the United States, were interested in our success. This made the local authorities very cooperative. The town temporarily donated to us an

The Jewish Students Association, in Heidelberg, around 1947.

empty two-story building with a garden outback that had served as a Jewish community center before the Nazis' ascent to power. As our headquarters, it was the site of many dinners and meetings, study sessions, late-night discussions, and religious ceremonies.

Marcel Tuchman, an organizing extrovert, was the leader and one of the founders of the association. His mother had been gunned to death in 1942, but he and his father had managed to survive the camp at Birkenau. His girlfriend, Shoshana, from Munkacs in Ruthenia, survived both Auschwitz and Bergen-Belsen. They were married on September 7, 1947.

Zygmunt Schwarzer, Marcel's classmate from Przemyśl, married Jean ("Szczepcia") from the same place. Both couples left for New York in 1949. Marcel would become a well known internist in the city and professor of medicine at New York University. Zygmunt succeeded as a pediatrician but fell ill and died prematurely.

Boris Anolik from Wilno in Polish Lithuania married Mina from Warsaw. They lived across the street from us on Mittermeierstrasse, and the alley was so narrow that we could open up our windows and easily converse with them across the gap. They moved early in 1949 to Florida, where he practiced pediatrics.

Nathan ("Natek") Wiener, a general practitioner, married Fanny and got settled in Haifa, Israel.

Gimpel Wajntraub, a gynecologist and obstetrician, got married in Israel and worked for many years at a major hospital in Jerusalem associated with Hebrew University. He was also widely known as a leading collector of ancient maps of Israel and the Middle East.

Stefan ("Pishta") Horenstein, from Hungary, specialized in gynecology, while his wife Lusia, from Poland, specialized in pediatrics.

Paul and Anna Ornstein were both from Hungary and specialized in psychiatry. The Ornsteins stayed in Heidelberg longer than others in our group, but eventually moved to Cincinnati, Ohio, to teach and do research.

Menek Goldstein, who survived hidden in a Polish village, became a brilliant chemist and neuroscientist. He developed tuberculosis while getting ready to board a ship for America in Bremen, and did important research at Basel, before continuing his career in New York.

Ernest Csendes (pronounced Chendesh) from Hungary, studied chemistry and worked in major industrial concerns in Europe and the U.S. Max Zając (Zayonts) married Kate (both from Poland). He studied linguistics and settled in Melbourne, Australia. Heimann, a student of philosophy, emigrated to Uruguay. Max Sprecher, a self-declared communist and student of Judaism, stayed in Heidelberg and lectured for some time in studies related to Talmud-Torah, but ended up finishing medicine. He was sometimes belligerent at our meetings, angrily defending Stalin and the Soviets. During these times, because I would speak up as someone who had stayed in the Gulag, my words carried weight. But the fanatical Sprecher would not be convinced.

We lost contact with Heimann and Sprecher, as well as two students of dentistry, one of whom moved to the French zone of Germany while another named Monias, from Poland, did well in Annapolis, Maryland.

Abe Shenitzer, a Holocaust survivor from Poland, studied mathematics. He made a fine career in research and teaching, first in the United States and then in Toronto, Canada. His books about great Russian mathematicians received much positive professional reception.

These friends and members of the Association of Jewish Students had all just gone through unbearable ordeals. Most were Polish concentration camp survivors. Lena and I, in fact, were the only ones who had been in Russia. We had all lost family members and were now trying to return to normalcy through our studies. Our community was like a family. Nothing could replace our losses, but this came as close as anything ever would. At no other time have I found so many kindred souls who could so easily relate to my experiences in life. It was a wonderful moment. There were so few Jews left in Germany, and yet we had somehow found each other at our time of greatest need.

Most of my friends were studying medicine. Like me, they planned to leave Germany as soon as they had taken their degrees because a person could practice as a doctor in any country. Unfortunately, my program of study—German Law—was not nearly so transportable. I had lost interest in law, and realized it was time to head toward a new direction. I had to find a universally applicable career in which a degree from a German university would be acceptable elsewhere also.

It was Marcel who first suggested economics. At first, I had some doubts. Ever since my school days in Łańcut I had excelled in humanities and faced more problems in mathematics. Moreover, I knew that the field of economics was littered with ratios, figures, and statistics. Soon, however, I took some courses and got converted. Professor LeCoutre taught economics of the firm, Sultan taught public finance, and Waffenschmidt lectured on money and banking. But, the leading figure in Heidelberg's faculty was Erich Preiser, a renowned author of books on economic theory, policy, history, and current events.

For me, as a student, his classes were more important than his writings. And he was a magnificent and rare lecturer, who spoke fluently and simply, and never seemed to resort to his notes. Germany, after the isolation of the Nazi years, had fallen behind the latest trends in economics—and in other sciences, too—but Preiser had many international contacts and always gave the impression of being *au courant*. He was friendly and encouraging. Over the next five years he would become, successively, my main teacher, counselor, mentor, and *Doktorvater*, or chairman of my doctoral dissertation committee.

Born in 1900, Preiser had studied economics in Frankfurt am Main during the 1920s. His own *Doktorvater* had been professor Franz Oppenheimer, a classical liberal who showed some socialist leanings. Preiser's dissertation dealt with Marx's theory of crises; he was one of the few real experts on Marx who did not consider himself a Marxist. In 1928, he had received his doctorate *summa cum laude*, with Oppenheimer heading up his committee. Preiser was teaching at the university in Jena in 1945, when the Russians occupied the city. He underwent lengthy interrogations at their hands before being released. Since no nation was more strict than the Soviets in their policy of denazification, the fact that they had let him go was ample proof that he was untainted by any hint of Nazism.

After a few of his enthralling lectures I became an enthusiastic student of economics. Unfortunately, I began with a serious disadvantage, having never read any of the fundamental texts of my new subject. When I was a young child, my father had seen that I was a promising scholar. Now, I fulfilled this promise. The next years were spent in a frenzy of studying. To catch up, I read for many hours a day, and often sat in the university library for long into the night. I believed my experience in the war had made me a better student. Before, learning had come easily to me. In Kraków, I had received good marks, but I hadn't given it my all. In Heidelberg, I was more serious. I had matured and I knew how precious an opportunity I had.

Still, all the maturity in the world wouldn't have sufficed if Lena hadn't been such an accommodating wife. In Ili, she had impressed me by juggling her many responsibilities with ease. Now she did the same, handling the housework, most of the responsibilities of childcare, and at the same time working toward her own master's degree in history.

In the mornings, she would prepare rolls with butter and jam for breakfast. While I studied, she would do the shopping in the busy markets on Bahnhofstrasse. Though we lived in Heidelberg, we were still eligible for our rations from the displaced persons camp. Once a month or so, I would ride the train to Bensheim and bring back groceries. During the winter, a coal truck would stop at our house and deliver fuel to heat the apartment. With this help, we were able to live comfortably. In the evenings, we would usually go on delightful walks, pushing Steven in his pram along the town's beautiful tree-lined streets.

Victor and Lena pushing son Steven along the streets of Heidelberg in the late 1940s.

We attended some great theater, such as Ibsen's *Gespenster*, (*Ghosts*) and some great music such as a memorable interpretation of Bruckner's "Romantic" (Fourth) symphony by an orchestra conducted by Wilhelm Furtwängler. On weekends, we could either hike in the mountains or sunbathe by the river. We spent many, many afternoons on the banks of River Neckar. We would swim, play, and row in rented sculls with friends.

At first, Lena and I had been the only married couple in the group. The other weddings began in 1947, and Steven remained the only child, who was spoiled rotten by our friends. Once, he hid in the garden behind the house. Marcel and I, who were responsible for keeping an eye on him, searched frantically but couldn't find him. I imagined telling Lena the horrible news, but was greatly relieved by the sight of Steven emerging from behind a bush, pleased with his prank, and beaming with delight.

He was strong and healthy, but one time he developed a nasty whooping cough. Our doctor suggested the local cure—fresh mountain air. So, every day for several weeks my son and I rode the cable railway to Königsstuhl, at the summit of mountains that overlooked the town. There we beheld a beautiful panorama: the river, mountains, and the town. Moreover, as an added bonus, his cough disappeared. Another incident was far more frightening. I was holding him in our apartment when he wriggled out of my arms and fell to the floor. Terrified, I ran with him all the way to the city hospital. He was fine, but I had the scare of my life, mitigated by the lucky fact that Lena was not around.

If, on the surface, our domestic lives seemed normal with the usual share of felicity, scrapes, and scares, we nevertheless never forgot that we were Jews living in Germany in the aftermath of World War II. The first thing I noticed was the total absence of Nazis. Suddenly, there were no Nazis to be found anywhere. The Germans were polite and accommodating, almost overfriendly.

The Americans were relatively lenient with their former enemies, prosecuting only the well-known Nazi officials. The Nuremberg Trials, which we followed in the newspapers, were being held far away in another part of the country, and didn't affect us directly. In Heidelberg, there were U.S. troops everywhere. Around the town, there were signs showing which clubs and other "unsavory" places were off-limits for the GIs (World War II veterans). Reputed to be a highly disciplined people, many Germans had now turned from pro- to anti-Nazis, though some appeared to be demoralized by defeat and unconditional surrender.

I took classes with young Germans and obviously they had been in the army. Clearly, many of the professors and administrators had cooperated with the Hitlerites. Nevertheless, it was not something that was discussed. I didn't become friendly with many Germans, but I had some acquaintances. I chatted in class with one former soldier. He had a motorcycle and once gave Steven a ride through the streets.

In 1948, after Marcel and I were elected as leaders of the Jewish Students Association, we were once invited for a meeting with the rector of the university, professor of theology, Dr. Freiherr von Kampenhausen. He wanted to know why we remained as a separate entity, instead of joining the Foreign Students Association. It seemed to him that we were bound by common sufferings but only perpetuating the old fears and hurts by keeping our distance. We told him that our group was also bound by positive characteristics of Jewish tradition and our own experiences. He liked to hear that and agreed.

Although unusually protected, we were inevitably immersed in a profoundly alien environment. In our daily lives, we were mostly happy to leave the Nazi era behind as if it was nothing more than an aberrant blip in German history. But at night, when we gathered together at the association's headquarters for dinner, we talked a lot about what was happening to us and what we were learning from our professors and acquaintances. What were the real chances for progress in Germany? In the world? What is left for us to do?

The one German with whom I could speak freely was Professor Preiser. He told me how he had developed a relationship with his own mentor, Professor Oppenheimer, and how, by the time he earned his degree, the two men and their wives had developed genuine personal friendships. It seemed likely that he and his wife, Änne, were inviting, perhaps even grooming Lena and me for a parallel relationship. We occasionally were guests at their home, where we often talked about the war. The fact that we had been under the Soviets instead of the Germans probably made it easier for us to establish a close friendship.

I felt that there was a real continuum between Oppenheimer, Preiser, and me. It was a valuable legacy and I was honored to be included with such eminent names. It wasn't until later that I learned just how symmetrical it was: it turned out that Oppenheimer himself had been a Jew.

As we worked out these issues amongst ourselves, German society at large was attempting to come to terms with its own past, too. First and the most ardent proponent of this was an eminent professor of philosophy in Heidelberg—Karl Jaspers. Shortly after the war, he had asked his students to honestly look at themselves. "The world indicts Germany and the Germans," he had said,

A few Germans admit their own guilt; most Germans hold themselves guiltless. Yet we Germans must seek the truth. We cannot be indifferent to what the world thinks of us, for we know we are a part of mankind—we are human before we are German. The guilt question is more than a question put to us by others, it is one we put to ourselves.[7]

At first the response was silent and hostile, but he continued to speak on the subject during 1945, 1946, and 1947. Lena and I attended some of his lectures at the Aula and followed the progress of his theory, which became known as "collective guilt." Jaspers carefully divided guilt into separate levels and came to the conclusion that, though Hitler's Germany was responsible for beginning the war, it was "nonsensical to charge a whole people with a crime." Nevertheless, he urged individuals not to hide from the past but rather to look inside their souls and acknowledge the role their nation had played in the atrocities of the Holocaust.

Jaspers was ahead of his time, and would eventually leave Germany to teach in Switzerland. To me, his arguments had immediate appeal. As a Jew living in Germany I was exposed to hatred. I could revel in the poverty in which the war had sunk the German people, not just gloat over their defeat (which I and all my friends did). My relatively advantageous position might have been called justice, but it was a stretched sort of justice: those who suffered were not necessarily those who were guilty of any crimes.

But some of my friends could not escape their hatred. For those who had been in the concentration camps, life among the Germans was especially difficult. Karol Targownik, an Auschwitz survivor whose wartime labor had been to remove corpses in the camp, was understandably irritable and often erratic. Once, in a streetcar, he almost attacked a passenger who rushed to take a place for which I had been waiting. The young man immediately surrendered his seat as the whole car looked on. Karol was triumphant, but I was mortified.

For all of that, Karol specialized in psychiatry, apparently with good results. He later worked in the well-known Menninger Clinic in Topeka, Kansas, and held a responsible position in advising the governor of the state. But he had a very unhappy first marriage as he divorced his first wife who openly became hostile to him, then he developed Alzheimer's disease, and was killed in a murder-suicide pact by his second wife, who loved him.

I myself have also suffered. I began experiencing a particularly upsetting recurring nightmare. In this dream, I was always surrounded by knives. Nothing ever happened; no one was murdered. It was just knives lying around and I was somehow involved with them, though I didn't necessarily do anything with them. I couldn't tell what these visions meant, but they bothered me extremely. It was natural for me to suspect that they were related to my losses from the war. The dreams dredged up thoughts that I, like so many other survivors, would have to grapple with for the rest of my life: why had I outlived the war, while my friends and family had perished? Had I done enough to help them?

I never mentioned the dreams to Lena, but the nighttime disturbances only grew more frequent and disturbing. So I started seeing a German psychoanalyst, Dr. Maria Giwjorra, at the main hospital in town. I would sneak out of the house each week to see her, lay on the couch in her office, and tell her my story. She was interested in my early life, while I was sure that my neurosis stemmed from the war years. Neither of us ever managed to fully interpret the dreams, but just talking about my problems was very helpful, and eventually the knives ceased tormenting me in the night.

It was Professor Preiser who first suggested that I write my dissertation on the Marginal Productivity Theory of Distribution, a complex economic theory that was fifty years old at the time, and still very controversial. Preiser, like so many German thinkers over the years, tended to favor theoretical work over the empirical business of gathering data and tallying results. Only time would tell, which of these tendencies I would favor, but in Heidelberg I was in no position to argue with the suggestions of my esteemed *Doktorvater*. So I weighed into the debate, applying the theory to the German economy, and the result was my dissertation: "The Theory of

Income Distribution: Development and Today's State." In German: "Die Theorie der Einkommensverteilung, Entvicklung und heutiger Stand." It was published as a book, which was not common in Germany at the time.

On May 18, 1951, I defended my work before a committee headed by Preiser himself, and was awarded my doctorate with the highest mark, *summa cum laude* ("with highest praise"). The dissertation was even printed as a book in the same year by J.C.B. Mohr, a publisher in Tübingen. I remember the great satisfaction I felt one day when I noticed my first book featured prominently in a display window of one of Heidelberg's best bookstores.

By this time, Marcel and his wife—and many others—had already left. With my studies done, it was time for us to leave, too. America was, by far, my first choice of destination, but my timing was bad. By 1951, nearly half a million displaced persons had already arrived in the United States, and the initial postwar generosity toward them had long since vanished.[8] Exacerbating this was the change in political climate, which, with the Cold War, had turned frosty. Anti-communist feeling had utterly twisted American attitudes toward displaced persons. If you were an immigrant in the early 1950s, it didn't matter if you had once been pro-Nazi as long as you were now anti-Soviet. Members of the Waffen SS ("Armed SS," literally meaning "Weapons SS") were being admitted, while anyone tainted by any contact with a socialist movement was barred.

Congress was debating the McCarran-Walter Immigration and Nationality Act, one of the most reactionary bills in American history, which put quotas on new arrivals and also allowed the government to deport immigrants deemed guilty of committing subversive acts. Anyone with any link with the Soviet Union was treated with suspicion. Unbelievably, this extended to the victims of the Gulag too, despite the fact that no one could be more anti-communist than those of us who had seen Stalin's system firsthand.[9]

We worked diligently to get our visas before this bill became law. Because of the presence of relatives and friends, as well as the prominence of the field of economics, America was our first choice of destination, but in light of the circumstances, we also completed emigration forms for Israel and Canada. I appealed for help to friends from Heidelberg who had already graduated and moved to the United States.

I had studied and admired *The Theory of Wages* by Paul Douglas, who was a U.S. Senator from Illinois, so I asked Marcel Tuchman and Abe Shenitzer to approach him on my behalf. They told him of my experiences in Poland and Russia and described my good record in studying economics in Heidelberg. The eminent economist and senator listened and graciously wrote a letter recommending that we be granted visas.

The summer and fall of 1951 passed in an atmosphere of uncertainty and apprehension. I earned some money by lecturing and conducting research at the University of Heidelberg, and commuted by streetcar to teach at the *Handelshochschule*, or Graduate School of Commerce, at nearby Mannheim. I also did some private tutoring of economic students and spent some time for this purpose in Switzerland. I joined the Horensteins, Ornsteins, and Bob and Jo Lewis in an excursion by car and on foot to the Bavarian Alps, where we roamed the mountains near Hitler's wartime retreat, the Eagle's Nest.

Finally, sometime late in 1951, just as it looked as if we had exhausted all available means without success, we got a lucky break. After one additional meeting with U.S. immigration officials in Ludwigsburg near Stuttgart, our application to enter the United States was granted and, indeed, sealed by a photograph in a local newspaper. Soon we fixed our departure for mid-January 1952, aboard the *U.S.S. General Taylor*, which was to sail from Bremen to New York.

The city of Bremen was still devastated but the port was ready and very busy. We arrived by train from Heidelberg a few days ahead of time and spent our remaining days in Europe trying to learn English in the displaced persons camp used as our quarters. During the night before our departure, Lena read Steven to sleep from Heinrich Hoffman's classic children's story "Struwwelpeter." The German tales are intended to frighten children into behaving. They describe child characters with bad habits who inevitably meet a bad end: cruel Friedrich, the "inky boys," Pauline's "utmost sad" playing with matches, and little thumb-sucking Kaspar who would not have any soup. We were going to a new world and Lena was determined that our family should make a good impression.

On the day our ship raised anchor, it was packed full of passengers and a small crew, the weather was cold and clear, and everybody seemed very happy. The ship was small and old, and had been used to transport world war troops.

The voyage started well but soon a near-disaster happened in the form of a violent storm that lasted for a full ten days and nights. The huge waves tossed the ship up and down and around as if it was a toy. Literally all on board, not only the passengers but also the crew, suffered from motion sickness to some degree, many badly, with lot of dizziness and nausea. It was very difficult to stay below decks and withstand the furious motion of the ship and one's own body along with the suffocating atmosphere. So people were lying on the deck, crowded, desperately trying to hold on to anything firm, constantly splashed and whipped by cascades of sea water. All three of us were sick to our stomachs, distressed, and cold, but we stayed on deck almost all the time. The struggle seemed very uneven and hopelessly biased in favor of the ocean and against our ship, which seemed to last forever, as the waves would never cease pounding and the wind would never stop howling.

However, as even the worst winter storms in the Atlantic do not rage forever, ours also ceased just as suddenly as it started. As soon as our battered ship encountered the Gulf Stream, the weather cleared up completely. The air got calm and fresh, reflecting the warm ocean current. The last two days of our crossing turned out to be just beautiful, and all of us enjoyed them fully, to make up for the preceding ordeal.

Not surprisingly, the entire passage reached its high point on the last day, January 31, 1952, when the *General Taylor* entered New York harbor. All newcomers rushed to the port side of the ship to watch the Statue of Liberty. No other sight ever moved me so deeply as this symbol of mankind's highest aspirations, particularly this first time. All of us felt happy and elated, including Steven, who, being while very young, absorbed ideas and impressions precociously. The ship then moved slowly north, getting close to the towering skyscrapers of Manhattan, looking at the modern bridges, cruising up the Hudson river, and finally berthing at one of the big midtown docks.

In those days, reporters were always present when a ship arrived, and somehow they had been told about me. It was not everyday that a displaced person arrived who happened to have a doctorate from Heidelberg. A newspaper photographer took a picture of the three of us, which turned out beautifully. Lena and I look joyfully at the approaching land and the crowd, while Steven is characteristically serious and seems lost in thought.

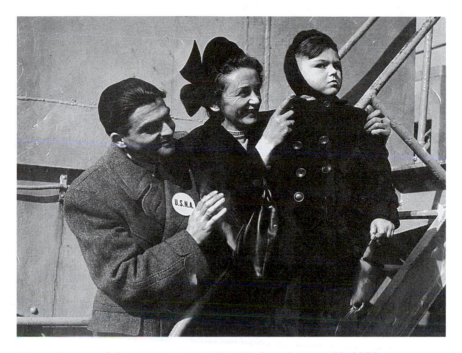

Victor, Lena, and Steven arriving in New York on January 31, 1952.

We are all dressed in our best. Lena looks handsome in a fine hat and is smiling happily.

Marcel and Abe were already waiting for us there, and we had a joyful reunion. After the formalities, we were taken to a small hotel assigned to some of our ship's passengers, which was at West 23rd Street, near the intersection of Broadway and Fifth Avenue. Our hotel catered to streetwalkers and other shady types, but we were too "green" yet even to recognize it, and too engrossed in our new environment to care. The windows of a large toy store on 22nd Street featured a magnificent railroad train traveling fast in a large circle. It fascinated Steven and myself. Unfortunately, we could only watch it long and intently, for we had little money left and none to spend on luxuries like those fabulous toys.

Life around us teemed with novelties and the New Yorkers seemed amazingly animated and self-absorbed. I soon sensed the openness, individualism, and tolerance—to me, the most attractive and enduring qualities associated with America, and particularly New York.

Our American Education

8 ■ ■ ■ We had come to the New World with some delay but still at a particularly opportune time. Europe was finally free of its worst totalitarian and criminal regimes but at the cost of a war that impoverished and exhausted the continent. By early 1952, it was apparent that America was fast becoming the richest and most powerful country in the world. More importantly, it was the only truly liberal one. It was the main place to be for an economist. The coming age would be as uplifting as the previous one had been devastating, and against long odds I would be able to see and participate in it.

But our very first necessity was finding an apartment. Luckily, others had gone through this process before us. My uncle Heinrich's daughters, Ella and Trudy, had been in America since before the war. I had never met them in Vienna, because when I had stayed with their parents there in 1938, they had both been vacationing with their husbands. Now they and their husbands—Fred Wind and Max Guth—lived in upper Manhattan's historic Washington Heights district, an area so crowded with Jewish refugees from Germany that it was jokingly referred to as the Fourth Reich.

Fred had prospered, becoming a co-owner of two men's clothing stores in midtown, and his wife took care of the apartment and their young daughter, Joyce. Max manufactured leather belts. Trudy, who along with Ella had learned the furrier trade from their father, worked in fine Manhattan fashion stores and was always very energetic. Her daughter Irene, was about nine at the time.

Trudy and Ella found us a rent-controlled apartment on West 173rd Street, which was near their own apartments. There was a bedroom for us and one for Steven. The rooms might have seemed a little dark at times, but across the street was a little tree-lined park with a stunning view of the Hudson river and George Washington Bridge.

Having secured a place to stay, we now needed to find jobs. Lena found one quickly in a hospital downtown. According to our immigration agreement, I was supposed to take a position in Cleveland, Ohio, but our family and friends all wanted us to stay in New York, which was also our own strong preference. So I found myself under great pressure to find work here as soon as possible. Although in a pinch I would take any reasonable job, I really wanted something in economics that looked promising. I searched for more than a month, whenever I had a spare moment. I prepared and sent out copies of a curriculum vitae, but it may not have been properly phrased and did not bring results. I walked the streets of midtown, visiting the offices of leading economic and business research organizations and asking for an interview. I was persistent, but had no success.

All this time my English was getting better. When I came to America I was able to read the language fairly well. But, since most of my reading had come in the course of my dissertation research, my vocabulary was weighted toward arcane terms of economic jargon, which were rarely useful in daily discourse. I improved like all other immigrants improve, through constant use. Trudy enjoyed showing us the town, and we talked English during these excursions and shopping trips. I didn't study in any systematic way, but read books, listened to the radio, and went to movies. I had taken several years of Latin and was fluent in German, and between these two languages I knew the roots to the majority of English words.

I was a quick study, and Lena was even quicker. But quickest of all was Steven. He was a smart child and right from the beginning he did well in his new school, P.S. 173. He was eager to assimilate, and he seemed to learn English and forget his German at about the same rate. In the evenings, we talked with him, and he became our most valuable teacher. It annoyed him when we spoke in Polish, because he assumed—often correctly—that we used that language when we wanted to keep secrets from him. Before long, we were speaking English at home. After a month I was largely fluent, but there was still the question of a job.

At first I made a little money by writing pieces in Polish for "Voice of America," but that was just a temporary expedient. Then my old professor, Erich Preiser, offered me a job teaching at a new university being founded in Regensburg. With genuine respect and regret, I declined this generous offer. Writing in Polish for the radio and teaching in a German university were both jobs that were rooted in the Old World. I had taken the voyage across the Atlantic to start a new life, and I wanted to find work that was based in America. I wanted to look forward to the future, not to spend my life examining the past.

In mid-March 1952, six weeks after our arrival, I had the lucky break that would shape the next fifty years of my career. After visiting dozens of other institutions during the previous weeks, I rode the elevator to one of the top floors in a high-rise on Columbus Circle, and stepped out into the headquarters of the National Bureau of Economic Research (NBER). Of all the organizations I had canvassed, the NBER was among those that I particularly esteemed. The group led the field in studying business cycles, and its reputation was such that I had read much of its literature all the way back in Heidelberg. I knew that this was where I wanted to work.

To be sure, I had no way of knowing that a temporary staff member from a university in Canada, Gideon Rosenbluth, had a position to fill. He was interviewing applicants to find an assistant to work on a new research project. I not only talked with him, but also with two older well-known NBER economists, George J. Stigler, then from Columbia University, and Geoffrey H. Moore, then associate director of Research. Despite my halting English, I did my best to tell them about my studies, dissertation, and scientific interests. Then, after a few days of nervous waiting, I received a positive reply inviting me to join Gideon's study of business concentration, mergers, and acquisitions.

This rather dry-sounding assignment represented an amazing opportunity, and I knew it. For my family, it was a time for reflection and thanksgiving. And, beginning at sundown on April 9, 1952, as Passover began, Jews all over the world joined us. Moses' escape from Egypt had rarely seemed more relevant, particularly to those of us who had managed to survive the Nazis' reign. Yet, even seven years after the war, thousands remained behind. New York synagogues shipped parcels containing Seder food to desperate families in Europe, where 75,000 Jews still awaited permission to flee to countries of sanctuary.[1] But for us, it was a Passover of celebration, of taking yet another step away from the bondage of our own recent past.

That week, I was contacted by a rabbi who was hosting a show on a local TV station. One of the reporters who had met our ship on the dock must have told him about our story, because the rabbi invited me and my family to come to the studio and participate in a staged Passover Seder that would air during the holiday. Each network was promoting some version of a Passover show; WABD was showing "The Four Questions," and WOR-TV had "The Freedom Story."[2] The program I was in featured a panel discussion followed by a ritual Seder.

I was to play the role of the recent immigrant who had come to America to find opportunity and freedom. This was a part I was qualified to play— since it was entirely true. I was probably one of the few newcomers who could boast a Ph.D., and so, to the producers, I was a shining example of promise and possibility. We went to the studio and rehearsed our lines. The host was going to ask me several questions about my life. I would look into the camera and talk about Oświęcim, the Gulag, and losing members of my family. Then, I was to tell of my time of recovery and renewed education in Heidelberg. Finally, I would describe my journey to America, and my happiness at being here. It was not hard to draw it out of me, as I was an enthusiastic immigrant and happy to talk.

The lights snapped on. The cameras started. The other speakers on the panel described their own stories, tragic and painful, uplifting and edifying. I think I was less anxious than most people would have been. Having only just seen my first television set on arrival in New York, I had no idea of its power and popularity. I didn't know enough to be nervous. Then it was my turn, and the microphones swung around to me. I answered the questions in English, as we had practiced, and it all went reasonably well. It might have been funny to think that just three months after my arrival I was already being held up for the American viewing audience as a success story. I knew, of course, that there were others who had suffered more and had survived who were now thriving, too. Nevertheless, it was a proud moment for me, and a kind welcome to America, where, after all, everyone wants to be on TV.

By the time of the Passover show, I had already been at the NBER for several weeks and had seen enough to understand the institution a little better. The NBER has been founded in 1920, during the early years of the field, and its original mission was to establish some basic, unbiased facts about the American economy, a goal, which at the time seemed like a novel idea. In that era, there were plenty of economic theories, but they were all based on generalities and guesses. No one, and no government agency, had ever taken the time to tally the American economy, and the NBER's first goal became the "determination of the distribution of national income among individuals and families, as well as by basic sources — wages and other returns for personal service, land rents, interest and profits."[3]

There was no doubt of the significance of these statistics. "A knowledge of this distribution is of vital consequence in the consideration of almost every important political and social problem," the NBER founders wrote.[4] The problem was how to conduct the research, which was at once so valuable and at the same time so easy to manipulate. In response, the Bureau stressed objectivity and scientific rigor. Its original board of directors consisted of a wide variety of economists, but each one was known to have a "judicial temperament," and agreed that their new institution was to be concerned, "wholly with matters of fact, and is being organized for no other purpose and with no other obligation than to determine the facts and to publish the findings."[5]

The Bureau's first assignment proved as difficult as predicted. To tally even a rough sketch of the nation's income distribution took two entire years, but when the results were issued as well as all the statistics the researchers had amassed, it was clear that a new and better method of economic investigation had been discovered. This first report eventually led to the annual recording of the Gross National Product (GNP). Within a decade, the NBER was supplying the U.S. government with most of its statistics about its own economy. But, as promised, it simply recorded the data while making no attempt to influence policy.

When I arrived thirty years later, this was all ancient history and the NBER was an established presence in the economics landscape. That's not to say that it was a luxurious place to work. My opening monthly salary of $200 was typical for the Bureau, which remained a nonprofit research organization where newcomers like me were paid low incomes. Because of my family's rent-controlled apartment and Lena's paycheck, this was just enough to cover the bills as well as our very modest needs and expenses. The great inflation of the post-World War II era, still at an early and very moderate stage, was soon to gather steam. But wages and salaries grew even faster for most employees along with the progress in technology and productivity, and we, at least, never felt poor or in the mood to complain.

I had always enjoyed an academic challenge. In Heidelberg, I had eagerly committed myself to catching up on my economics reading, taking graduate-level courses despite never having studied the subject before. In New York, once more, I basically had to start over again. The NBER was the leading institution for the study of business cycles. While I had learned a little about this complex branch of economic theory with professor Preiser, I was by no means up to NBER standards. So, my first months at the Bureau were spent in a frenzy of catching up. It wasn't simply a question of reading books either, I had to learn an entirely new method of thinking about the science of economics.

Preiser was a brilliant theorist, but like so many leading German intellectuals in history his theories tended to be speculative and idealistic. The NBER way of conducting business was as different from this as possible. It was a very American organization, in the sense that it had been founded to achieve an incredibly ambitious goal—no less than the quantification and analysis of all income and wealth in the United States—and it was determined to be as scientific as possible. There would be no room, or at least very little room, for theory.[6] In fact, in 1947, one of the NBER's most famous opponents, the Nobel Prize-winning economist T.C. Koopmans charged that the Bureau practiced "measurement without theory." This accusation wasn't really true and, anyway, relying on data wasn't necessarily a bad thing in a field where there were a multitude of theories pointing in different directions, often contradicting one another.

Creating a theory is often viewed as a higher calling than the unglamorous labor of collecting facts; it is considered more cerebral, more mysterious, and more elegant to identify causes, which is the goal of a theory, than to simply identify the real-world effects of economic indicators. But, I disagreed with this thinking. I always saw raw facts as the basis for all analysis, so I liked NBER's skeptical view of abstract theories. I liked no less their insistence on patient gathering of good data and careful testing of relevant theories in the light of evidence. I found that the Bureau's way of doing things meshed perfectly with my own preferences.

I embraced the NBER style and felt liberated by the experience, though it once led me into an awkward situation. After Preiser died I found myself at a party talking with his widow. She talked about his career and his various brilliant theories. Then she turned to me and rather pointedly said, that since I had been one of his students surely I wasn't one of those vulgar empirical economists, but rather valued the elegance of theoretical thought. Without offending, I gently corrected her assumption: with all due respect to my former professor, I had indeed become one of *those* economists. For me, and others like me, there was no place like the NBER.

After about a year and a half, I had gone a certain way toward establishing myself as one of the promising young researchers at the Bureau, but I realized that I would need additional training in order to truly become up-to-date with the latest ideas in American economics. I applied to the Social Science Research Council (SSRC), an independent nonprofit organization, which had been supporting training for younger researchers since 1923, and received a postdoctoral research training fellowship. With that money I was able to spend the 1953–1954 academic year in Cambridge, studying at Harvard. As a research fellow, I had free choice of which courses to take and no other obligations but to study, write, and make the most of it. I attended Paul Samuelson's seminar at Massachusetts Institute of Technology (MIT) and Wassily Leontief's seminar at Harvard.

My interlude in Cambridge may have been valuable for my career, but it was disastrous for my family. Lena, after the nomadic lifestyle she had suffered through for years, had finally felt settled in New York, where she had family and friends. The costs of living in Massachusetts were less than in New York and our income was about the same, but we could not find as good and affordable an apartment to live in as our rent-controlled place in the city. We ended up staying in a rather small and shabby building above a shoe store near a crowded business square. Lena, who had grown up with wealth, remained very sensitive to living conditions and, without admitting it, probably resented the move away from the city and people we had all come to like so much.

Indeed, after some time, Lena fell seriously ill, took an overdose of aspirin pills, and was taken to a nearby hospital with an undiagnosed nervous condition. The cause was never exactly diagnosed, but no doubt it was due in part to the stresses and losses she had suffered in the war years. I had gone through a similar breakdown in Heidelberg, when I had been tormented by nightmares. Lena had stayed strong throughout that whole period, and had seemed to flourish in New York. But this latest move was one too many. She was transferred to the large Massachusetts General Hospital across the Charles River in Boston. There she gradually recovered but not without having undergone two electric shock treatments for which my consent was not sought.

It was a terrible time for us. At times I almost felt as if I were losing my mind. I was stricken with guilt and asked myself the same questions over and over: we had finally found a good apartment in the great city in which we wanted to live, I had started a modest but interesting and promising job; why had I been so impatient for more and forced us to leave all this after just a little over a year?

Steven had been upset at leaving his school, and he was unhappy about mother's illness and absence. I remember one night when I read him a sad fairy tale by Hans Christian Andersen about a little fir tree. The tree loved the forest, sun, and birds. It longed to grow tall but was cut down young, enjoyed briefly the splendor of being bedecked with glittering ornaments and toys, but after Christmas it was discarded, withered, and decayed. Steven usually showed little emotion and was outwardly sunny, but at the end of this story he wept bitterly. That night, I had a hard time trying to hide my own tears.

Luckily, Lena was young, hopeful, and resilient. The academic year ended on a high note with the completion of my first paper in English. "Causes and Consequences of Changes in General Equilibrium Systems" had originated in Leontief's input–output seminar, and was later published in the British journal, *Review of Economic Studies*. We returned to New York in the summer of 1954 and Lena's health improved quickly. We were lucky to get another affordable apartment in Washington Heights and Steven was reunited with friends and happy again in the nearby school.

I returned to work at the NBER. While I was away at Cambridge, the Bureau had moved from Columbus Circle to Madison Avenue near 39th Street. But that wasn't the only change I came to appreciate. My year as a research fellow—taking courses and workshops, conversing, reading, and writing—had improved my English dramatically. Now I made friends with several young research associates at the Bureau, all of whom also taught at nearby colleges and universities. These included Phil Cagan, Dan Holland, Tom Juster, Harry Kahn, Phil Klein, Bob Lipsey, and Ralph Nelson (in business cycles, money and banking, government finance, consumption, international economics, and mergers and acquisitions). I soon started teaching macroeconomics at Columbia University's outlet for continuing education, the School of General Studies. I also had a chance to interact with my colleagues at the annual meetings of the American Economic Association (AEA) in Detroit (1954) and in New York (1955). These meetings, usually held between Christmas and New Year, offered an important opportunity for economists, particularly the younger ones, to meet each other and their seniors.

I had finally caught up with the American way of studying the science of economics. No longer did I feel out of my depth, or uneasy with the language. I was ready to really begin my career. My first joint article with a NBER staff member was "Cause and Consequence of Retailers' Buying" coauthored with Ruth P. Mack and published in the March 1958 issue of *The American Economic Review*. Geoff Moore, one of the top economists at the Bureau, had liked the paper and some unpublished notes I had written at Harvard. I soon started to work with him on a two-volume collection of essays entitled *Business Cycle Indicators*, which would eventually be published by the Princeton University Press.

The study of business cycles then became the main focus of my career. My research with Moore in the 1950s would contribute to the development of the present-day lists and indexes of leading, coincident, and lagging indicators of business cycles in the United States and several other countries. These are specific accomplishments, perhaps only understandable to other economists. But, what we were attempting to achieve eventually was as scientific and reliable a system for predicting future economic trends as feasible. The value of this could hardly be doubted. A businessman who has good reasons to believe that the economy will continue to boom will invest in the growth of his company. A government who foresees a recession will prepare to alleviate the pain its citizens will feel.

Of course, predicting the future is an inexact science. Really, it is more of an art form. No single variable, not even the best known and most comprehensive, such as the Gross Domestic Product (GDP), can alone represent what's going on or predict what's coming. Economies are based on people, and people don't always behave rationally. Therefore, to be practically relevant, and not just formally elegant, our models have to recognize human diversity and limitations. Economists learned how to create models of highly efficient markets that worked perfectly and predictably, but experience made me doubt the value of assuming that people act as if they were equipped with superior skills and foresight. My time in the Soviet Union had convinced me of the impossibility of controlling a planned economy with all its complexity, vagaries, and whims. In a market economy, forecasters have no constant and reliable model of economic performance; they can just try to anticipate and comprehend it over time.

The attempt to understand business cycles, that is to say, sequences of expansion and contraction, was itself among the more complex and difficult assignments ever tackled. Why do economies suffer recessions even while generating long-term growth as millions of people go to work to create useful goods and services that other people buy? Yet, along with others at other times and elsewhere, we economists at the National Bureau found long and good evidence that business cycles persisted in modern market economics over great many decades. The fluctuations, while nonperiodic, were recurrent. Despite all the changes in technology, tastes, and international events, the average durations over successive subperiods of several decades retained some similarity (about four years in the United States and five in Europe).

The intermediate and longer trends in the economy are represented by time series of important economic and financial indicators. These are measures of critical aspects of general economic performance, which together form both the instruments and the targets of forecasting. They are discussed everyday in the business pages and on TV. I played an active part in creating some of them. My 1973 monograph: *Orders, Production and Investment—a Cyclical and Structural Analysis* showed that many goods are manufactured to order. Hence, for them the change in unfilled orders and the level of new are useful predictors of changes in output and shipments. In particular, the important part of these advance orders and contracts refers to investment commitments, which track business purchases of plant and equipment. Such investments in factories, machinery, equipment, and so on, represent major decisions amidst much uncertainty and long planning.

Our second son, Arthur Harvey (Chaim in Hebrew, after my wife's father) was born in New York on July 25, 1958. Lena was close to forty and I was very nervous during that long night, waiting at the Knickerbocker Pavilion of the Mount Sinai Medical Center at 100th Street and Fifth Avenue. Some of the time I was at her side, but when the scene was too intense; I was taken to wait outside with the other anxious expectant fathers. Steven told me he was nervous too and was up all night. He passed the time by reading *The Count of Monte Cristo*. But all went well and mother and baby soon came home.

This was a great family event. We wanted the baby very much and rejoiced as it grew and flourished. My cousins, Ella and Trudy, still lived nearby and helped. Steven, who was almost twelve, had to get used to sharing his parents' attention with Artie, at the time the more demanding partner.

With a new baby at home, we had less opportunity to sample the city's incomparable cultural scene, but we still found some time to appreciate world-class music and theater. We could afford only a very few nights out before our return from Cambridge, but as my salary increased, we became regular patrons of the arts. I remember well our earliest concert in the Town Hall of mid-Manhattan. Jesse Weil, a New York lawyer who had befriended and helped us in Heidelberg, joined us at the performance. It featured the beautiful score for Aaron Copland's *Rodeo*. Giuseppe Verdi's magnificent *Don Carlo* and *Aida* were the only operas we attended at the old Met (Metropolitan) at Broadway and 39th Street, before the Met's move to Lincoln Center in 1966. Of those performances, the most memorable was that of Princess Eboli sung by mezzo Grace Bumbry while Steven admired Renata Tebaldi as Aida.

Steven was again taking piano lessons. I attended a fine concert with him, in which Rudolph Serkin played Beethoven's "Emperor" piano concerto. We ran into Steven's piano teacher at this concert and had blintzes with her at the celebrated Russian Tea Room next door. In 1959, Steven had a bar mitzvah in a synagogue on Fort Washington Avenue near where we lived. By that time, he had finished elementary school and started commuting by subway to the Horace Mann School in Riverdale on 246th Street. Horace Mann was an exclusive private "country day" school. The all-boy school tried to pattern itself on English models. Steven was a good student and had been awarded a scholarship to attend it. He felt poor and badly dressed among students who arrived in limousines. We could afford attending only one of the benefit affairs for Horace Mann (a good concert at Carnegie).

Sometime in the autumn of 1958, I boarded a plane for Midway Airport on Chicago's South Side. I was heading to the Midwest for a job interview at the University of Chicago's Graduate School of Business, where they were reorganizing and recruiting new faculty. My flight passed through a horrendous storm, and after some terrifying moments we were diverted from our route and forced to make an emergency landing in Detroit. From there I enjoyed the secure tedium of train travel, with which I had been familiar from my earliest days. I arrived in Chicago safe and sound, but quite late.

I was interviewed by Dean W.A. Wallis, professor of statistics, Jim Lorie, and George P. Schultz, professor of labor economics who would soon be named the new dean (later, Schultz would become U.S. Secretary of Labor, and eventually Secretary of State). They readily forgave my tardiness, and they must have liked me, since I got invited to join the faculty as an associate professor of finance on a track for permanent tenure. I was impressed by the history of the school, which, having been founded in 1898 as the college of commerce and politics, was the second oldest business school in the country. Even more important were the school's plans for the future. An ambitious expansion was in the works, enrollment was to triple, millions were being spent on a new campus, and prominent economists were being wooed for the faculty.[7]

The most prominent professors were George Stigler, Ronald Coase, and Gary Becker in economics (who later earned Nobel Prizes in 1982, 1991, and 1992, respectively), Merton Miller in finance (who received the award in 1990), and Robert Fogel (winner of the 1993 Nobel Prize for studies in cliometrics, quantified economic, and business history). The school also attracted excellent students (Myron Scholes, whom I remember well from my own advanced macroeconomics class, shared the 1997 Nobel Prize for inventing an option pricing formula.) But the Nobel Prize only happens to be the best-known distinction; it may not always recognize the best work and is easily overstated. Certainly other faculty did no less excellent work, for example Sidney Davidson in accounting (he also served for a time as dean), Eugene Fama in finance, Arnold Zellner and Henri Theil in econometrics, Harry Roberts in statistics, John Gould (also a former dean) and Gary Eppen in business economics, Robert Aliber in international trade and finance, and Arnold Weber in labor.

With these bright stars either in place, or on their way, I was happy to accept the offer. After six years in New York City, the family was again on the move. In 1959, we arrived and rented an apartment on the third floor of an old six-flat building at the corner of 58th Street and Blackstone Avenue. We had to walk up three tall floors but had an affordable, spacious apartment. The living room and enclosed porch looked out over Blackstone Avenue, followed by our, Arthur's, and Steven's bedrooms. In the back there was the dining room and kitchen with an open porch overlooking the campus. There was a long hallway that linked all the bedrooms, which was why this was called a "railroad flat."

Ours was a pretty, tree-lined street and, by good luck—for none of us knew much about Chicago—it happened to be one of the better spots in the historic neighborhood known as Hyde Park. Both deans Schultz and Lorie lived on the same block of Blackstone Avenue. The campus, a mixture of neo-Gothic and modern buildings, and divided into quadrangles on both sides of the broad, park-like Midway Plaisance, was a walk of few minutes from our apartment.

We soon met our neighbors. Hirofumi Ozawa, a well-known professor of economics, before long chose to return to Japan, where he preferred to educate his children. The Lehnhoffs, he the principal violist of the Chicago Symphony, lived on the second floor. Under Fritz Reiner, the Symphony was becoming world famous, and with the introduction of stereophonic sound and the LP (long-playing phonograph record) a few years earlier, classical music recording was in its heydays. We had just bought our first stereo and Steven and I were beginning to collect classical records. I knew the music, but he was very interested in the quality of performance, especially for piano, and had strong opinions. Lester Telser, another young professor from the business school, who lived on Blackstone Avenue nearby, often joined me as we walked our baby carriages (I with Arthur, he with Joshua). Lena became friendly with several faculty wives, notably Frieda Davidson, Obie Schultz, Sylvia Telser, and Agnes Zellner.

We enjoyed a particularly close friendship with Arcadius Kahan, a professor of economic history in the Department of Economics, and his wife Pearl. He was from Wilno in the Lithuanian part of Poland, a Yiddishist interested in the economic history of the Jews in general and in Wilno, a great center of Jewish culture, in particular. We met many interesting people at their home, notably the great novelist Saul Bellow whose works I admired, and Jacob Frankel from Israel, later the governor of the central bank there. (Now the post is occupied by Stanley Fisher from Zimbabwe, in my time also a professor of economics in Chicago and a friend.) Unfortunately, Arcadius had a heart problem. We once drove him at night to the emergency room at the university hospital. He died young of a heart attack.

We developed much affection for our neighborhood, style, and routine of life and work. Unlike New York, a car is a necessity in Chicago. I learned to drive in 1960 and our first car was an inexpensive white Ford Falcon sedan. I remember buying it from Courtesy Ford and also remember that "friendly" Jim Moran was the television pitchman for the dealership. The price, exactly $999, would be the equivalent today of probably no less than tenfold that amount. The little car was tough to drive without power steering—you needed strength to turn the wheel, which is unknown today. Steven inherited this car in 1965. That year we moved up to a much more powerful Buick Skylark, which we all loved. We used it a lot, for vacations and long trips to Canada, New York, and California. Mainly we drove around Hyde Park and to the Loop. We took visitors on a scenic ride by Lakeshore Drive along Lake Michigan and then to the elegant city avenues and neighborhoods on the near north side. Many visitors enjoyed these tours and thanked us for them.

Hyde Park is considered an intellectual enclave because of the university. It is also a multiracial neighborhood that is not predicated on a dominant ethnicity. Other Chicago neighborhoods are noted, to the contrary, for a dominant nationality or group, such as the primarily Jewish commercial area and market on Maxwell Street or the Italian neighborhood south of the Loop on Taylor Street (now about as small as the remains of New York's "Little Italy"). Larger ethnic neighborhoods include the Polish neighborhood on the north side centered on Milwaukee Avenue and the large Jewish neighborhood on Devon Avenue on the far north side (now shared with Indians and Pakistanis).

All of us came to feel at home in Chicago and seemed to enjoy our life there, especially Lena. After two years at the university, I was granted tenure and a full professorship. I missed the National Bureau but found ways to continue working with them. Steven worked out the adjustment

Steven, Victor, Lena, and Arthur in Chicago in the early 1960s.

smoothly but always considered himself to be a New Yorker (he's still a Yankees fan after all these years). Arthur was too young to remember New York and knew only Chicago during his childhood.

The town's motto is "urbs in horto"—city in a garden—and a bird's eye view from a plane, which I have often enjoyed, confirms the boast. New York may be more cosmopolitan, Chicago more American, but both are great cities, dynamic, open, and always changing. They are both melting pots and centers of diversity. In both places, the atmosphere of liberty and tolerance, which is joined by economic and cultural demands, promotes assimilation. We were naturally receptive to this process, which accelerated when we moved to a more thoroughly "American" environment. Our troubles were fading into memory and all forecasts for the future seemed bright.

My American Century

9 ▪ ▪ ▪ In early 1957, after our prescribed five years in America, we all took the subway down to the Federal courthouse in lower Manhattan. Though in our late thirties, Lena and I felt young and hopeful. Steven, who turned ten a few months before, was a curious, smart, and happy youngster. In a large room, surrounded by other families, we listened to a judge give a patriotic exhortation on the virtues of America. He asked us to stand and raise our right hands. Then he recited the "Oath of Citizenship," and we repeated it. We had officially become U.S. citizens.

Yet, this was only true in the formal sense. In a deeper sense, we had been preparing for this moment during our whole stay in the country, and emotionally, even longer. At first, just being in America had been so different for us; all of our energy had gone to adjusting to our new life. We had immersed ourselves in the culture, reading newspapers and, increasingly, books, listening to radio, watching TV, and watching movies. More than those born here, we really had to scrutinize and study this country, before we could learn how to behave here, and eventually find our place. The five-year wait that immigration required seemed like the perfect period. By 1957, I felt truly ready to take up my life as an American citizen. The ceremony was just the official ratification of the process, but for me it was nevertheless a powerful moment—the most fulfilling moment, perhaps, of my entire political life, which until then was admittedly very limited.

In that respect, I was probably like other immigrants, but among others I stood out. Most came here to find a better life, and many were fleeing persecution in other countries, but few had known the degree of pain suffered by the Jewish immigrants of my generation. Having come from Poland, Russia, and Germany, and seen virulent racial and class hatreds at work in totalitarian regimes, I knew just how much better America was. To me this was the most promising country on earth. As all human creations have, it had its flaws, but I tried to understand and forgive them, if possible. My time here was to include some tumultuous years, political struggles that would test the nation's founding principles; but even at its most divided, the United States, in my opinion, could never be compared with Hitler's Germany or Stalin's Russia. People, who have only lived here, even including my own sons, can never have the perspective of those of us who survived the Gulag or the Holocaust. And hopefully, they never will.

Julius and Ethel Rosenberg were executed at Sing Sing in 1953, a little more than a year after we had arrived in New York. That was a terrible thing. We had followed the trial in the papers and were very upset by the government's course of action. Though I felt sorry for the Rosenberg family and was sure that their deaths were undeserved, I could never feel much understanding for American leftists who had such a sympathetic view of the Soviet Union. They had never seen it, had never lived there, and had no appreciation for the reality of life for the Russian people. The Americans, I think, created their own Soviet Union, an idealized place that could stand in opposition to the things in their own country with which they disagreed. I had lived in both countries and found no reason at all to doubt that the United States was far freer and happier overall. As an economist, I believed it was the competitive market system that provided more people with better opportunities.

As I was becoming a citizen in 1957, Senator Joseph McCarthy had just a few months left to live. His power had crested and receded the previous year after his vain attempt to attack the U.S. military. But the era that bears his name was hardly over. Anti-communism, sometimes extreme and irrational, was still the dominant political force in America. People were being forced to take loyalty oaths, not just to work for government, but also to participate in even the most mundane activities. As I was taking my "Oath of Citizenship," in Lower Manhattan, the City's Department of Water Supply was enforcing a law requiring loyalty oaths for those looking for fishing permits, worried, no doubt, that communist infiltrators were planning to contaminate or dynamite the reservoirs.[1]

Yet, the absurdity of such restrictions was for me, not a sufficient reason to oppose the policies of the United States. Even when critical of the government, I tended to believe in its goodness. I do not deny that this may have been a result of my experiences as a young man. It is possible that I have sometimes been too ready to forgive America's weaknesses because I am so conscious of its strengths.

In 1960, shortly after moving to Chicago, I cast my first vote for president. For most Americans voting probably seems like a natural right, and perhaps even an obligation. But immigrants who have become citizens can appreciate the act at its true value. When I was a kid I had revered charismatic Polish leaders, such as Marshal Piłsudski. I had even cheered Polish President Moscicki in the streets of Oświęcim. By 1960, when I was over forty years old, I had long since lost faith in political leaders. I agreed with Winston Churchill who once said, "democracy is the worst form of Government except all those others that have been tried." But it was still a thrilling moment for me when I cast my ballot for John F. Kennedy. After all, this was the first vote that I had ever cast in my entire life.

Politics had always been a secondary concern for me. I had been a studious child and a conscientious student. The 1960s, a turbulent time for many Americans, were among the most fruitful years of my career. My first publication after we moved to Chicago was "Index Numbers and the Seasonality of Quantities and Prices," written for *The Price Statistics of the Federal Government,* a large study for the Joint Economic Committee of the U.S. Congress directed by George Stigler (NBER 1961). This essay shows how complex and critical are proper seasonal adjustments for the valid measurement of business cycles (non-seasonal fluctuations in both quantities and prices). My work with Moore and others at the National Bureau of Economic Research (NBER) in dating U.S. recessions and recoveries resulted in several journal articles, "selected papers," published by the Graduate School of Business (GSB) of the University of Chicago, and issues of "Explorations in Economic Research," a new NBER quarterly.

My main interest remained focused on the growing field of analyzing business cycles. Even while the U.S. economy suffered from much wartime and political instability, it, on the whole, did well by defying inflation and continued to grow.

The widespread forecasts of a crash and depression to follow World War II (as the 1920–1921 crisis and deflation followed the first one) never materialized. The 1945 recession, due entirely to the war-to-peacetime transition, was short and relatively mild. A boom-bust cycle in U.S. exports and, to a lesser extent, a slowing of inventory investment caused a mild recession at the end of 1948 and through most of 1949. In 1953–1954, the economy experienced a moderate decline, which was attributable to the liquidation of the defense buildup after the end of the Korean War. Higher inflation and interest rates depressed investment and an easier monetary policy revived the economy in 1957–1958. Still another short and mild recession, due to a prior steel strike and tax hikes, occurred in 1960–1961.

The science of forecasting was new and people in the business world were excited by the prospect of taming the risks of sudden economic shifts. But it was soon clear that economic predictions were far from being up to the job of guiding a counter-cyclical stabilization policy. Most forecasters were surprised by each of the above-mentioned recessions. From 1953 to 1965, the average forecast had underestimated the growth in Gross National Product (GNP) by $7 to $12 billion each year,[2] and the President's Council of Economic Advisors' forecasts were rarely sufficiently accurate. "Businessmen and investors who follow forecasts have been warned to take the predictions of economists with a grain of salt," wrote a reporter for *The New York Times* in 1965,

The warning comes from Victor Zarnowitz of the University of Chicago, who is conducting a study of forecasting for the National Bureau of Economic Research. According to his preliminary findings, forecasters are generally off from 1.5 per cent to 2.5 per cent, a margin of error wide enough to make the difference between a boom and merely good business or between good business and a recession.[3]

Many newspaper reports referred to my research project for the NBER in the 1960s, in which we surveyed the work of hundreds of forecasters. The early economic forecasts had been relatively inaccurate, and I think that reporters were skeptical and eager to announce my critical findings.

In an article headlined, "Indicators or Hunches," a *Wall Street Journal* writer sneered:

Notwithstanding the growing number of sophisticated business forecasting tools from electronic computers to elaborate statistical indicators, the crystal ball seems to be getting no less cloudy. So far anyway. "An Appraisal of Short-Term Economic Forecasts," a recent study published by the National Bureau of Economic Research and prepared by University of Chicago economist Victor Zarnowitz, details the tarnished record of those who seek to divine the future.[4]

However, far from documenting the "tarnished record" out of spite, I was trying to point out areas for improvement. True, the record of predictions was not inspiring. The main weakness in the forecasts that I found was, not surprisingly, "that they've been poorer for longer future spans than for shorter. That is, they've been pretty good for one quarter-year ahead, not quite as good two quarters ahead, and progressively less accurate for longer periods ahead."[5] My conclusion acknowledged that there was a lot of work to do in this field. "The record," I wrote, "of forecasters in predicting turning points—changes in the direction of economic activity—is on the whole poor." Hence, our failings were centralized in the area where we needed to be the strongest. Since our models were based on past performance, they were rarely able to predict sudden changes—exactly the situations that businesses were most eager to predict.[6]

In addition to these studies for the NBER, I was also focusing on my lectures at the GSB of the University of Chicago. I taught basic macroeconomics, money and banking, and an advanced course in business cycles and forecasting. The first two courses (Bus 303 and Bus 331) were taken by students working to acquire the degree of a Master of Business Administration (MBA). The third course (Bus 403) was open to MBA students, too, but attracted mainly students in the doctoral (Ph.D.) programs in both the School of Business and the Department of Economics.

The faculty in Chicago competed in offering interesting, ambitious, and well-prepared courses and seminars. Students also competed for these courses by paying more from their allotment of points for the most popular classes and workshops. The school had a well-earned reputation for being a highly, even fiercely, competitive place. As a novice I found it difficult to attract students away from established stars in the required courses that were offered in several sections. Over time, I managed to get between thirty and sixty students in my sections of two basic courses, and up to twenty students in the optional advanced course. These numbers were good but not outstanding. Even so, I once estimated on the basis of the official registration figures that I must have had a total of several (perhaps at least five) thousand MBA students over my thirty years at the GSB, and a few hundred Ph.D. students.

I enjoyed teaching, especially classes with excellent students of whom there were many at Chicago, not only at the doctoral level but also the undergraduates who were taught by the faculty in the departments and graduate schools (I did some of that, too). I liked to stress in my lectures the need to advance understanding of two sides of our study subject. First, there are the important events and developments, factors and relationships from studies of macroeconomic and business cycle history. Second, there are the theories that fare well in tests using the corresponding data. I would not spend much time on other abstract theories, however elegant, which do poorly in the light of such tests. But I also tried to explain the important role in contemporary mainstream economics of equilibrium models based on the attractively simple and helpful hypothesis of utility and profit-maximizing behavior.

I found much understanding of my point of view, and even considerable sympathy with it, among students, although its representation among faculty was far from strong (later it gained ground gradually with the advent of "behavioral" economics). The assumptions of rational expectations and behavior lend much vigor to the general theory of how a market economy works, but extreme reliance on them produces unrealistic results.

At home, Lena and I proudly watched our boys grow up. We considered ourselves fortunate for being able to provide first Steven and then Arthur excellent educations, both in and out of school. They learned a lot about European and American history, cultures and art, and liked to know and talk about these matters. Growing up means looking forward, not backward, particularly in America. For Steven and Arthur, school always came first, without much supervision or prodding on our part (Lena was always the stricter parent). Their education was obviously a matter of great importance to all of us, and one of the main sources of Americanization of our family.

Steven was actually very interested in history, but to him it was similar to watching a long movie about strange people. He also did well in languages

(English and French). It would have been easy for him to excel in German if he had chosen it. He was an early and avid reader and especially liked historical novels (by now, he has read almost all of Dumas including the obscure adventures of Cellini at the court of Francis I, the page of the Duke of Savoy, and even the forgotten Chevalier d'Harmental). He also developed a great interest in and learned much about classical music and late-Medieval and Renaissance art.

I remember a visit to the Metropolitan Museum of Art in 1958 when Steven questioned the title of a Poussin painting. He received a thank-you note from the painting's curator, but it is not clear whether the painting's title was ever corrected as he suggested.

Arthur, on later trips to contemporary art museums in Chicago, New York, and Europe, told me what to look for and value in abstract art, about which I knew little. He was more visually oriented, even when very young, and liked modern art and rock music. His interest and taste in reading developed more slowly but became strong too, with preferences for adventure and contemporary fiction.

When we arrived in New York, television was beginning to compete with other media for news and to replace movies as the prime source for popular entertainment. Although going out to movies was a great pastime, it was both easier and cheaper to watch television. Both television and movies idealized an American lifestyle of freedom and wealth. The media showed families facing and resolving practical problems so that they could prosper. In totalitarian societies, propaganda revolved around loyalty and sacrifice for the good of the state and its ideas. Films about World War II and the heroism of American soldiers had dropped off at the end of the war and were to reemerge in more epic form in the early 1960s. Less pleasant movies about the Nazis and their war crimes were also to come later.

In any event, our previous lifestyles suffered by comparison with the American present. Envy of this country was worldwide, particularly at a time when much of Europe and Asia were still ruined by the war. However, the appreciation of the United States must have been particularly strong in the minds of people with our experiences.

For many refugees and other immigrants, embracing the new world was tantamount to dismissing the old as inferior and unjust (and utterly alien to the young). There was condemnation both of the perpetrators of the Holocaust and also its silent collaborators. The most extreme views of Europe's collective guilt risked throwing the baby out with the bathwater — a total rejection of the European prewar cultures as incriminated by the Holocaust.

I saw this as a pitfall to be avoided, and hoped most other people would agree. After all, the great cities of America, in which we were lucky to live, are the likely heirs of the great European culture before its decline in the mid-twentieth century.

We encountered TV first upon our arrival in New York, acquired a set as soon as we could afford it, and learned a lot about English and our new surroundings from the little screen. Televisions were relatively expensive, almost a month's wages. Steven was interested in westerns, like most small boys in the early 1950s, and begged us for a set. But along with the benefits there was also potential for harm, all of which soon became apparent with the rapid growth of the new industry and its programming. The proliferation of violence and vulgarity combined with the emptiness of excessive watching to create serious problems for parents and teachers. While they struggled with television for the attention of youth, other media struggled with television for the attention of the public at large.

In these contexts, television was generally the strongest, even against the motion picture industry. The solution for responsible families was not "laissez-faire" but strict supervision, enforcement of moderation, and choices of good programs: a strategy much recommended and discussed at the time and presumably widely followed. I feel that our own family did so with good results, in the main simply by not overdoing a good thing.

As our children grew, they came to know a good deal about what had happened to us and to our generation, even though we all avoided talking about it. Although we felt the need to deal with our past, and the Holocaust was becoming an important subject of public discourse, it was not an easy issue for us to discuss. Lena and I did not actively shield them from the details of our sufferings, but at the same time we didn't feel like subjecting them to the knowledge of what had happened to us. They understood why they had never met their grandparents, but I never sat them down on my lap and explained about my journey with Tadek across Poland, or our freezing days and nights in the Karelia Gulag. Looking back, I don't know whether I was protecting them, or myself.

One thing I did realize, though, was how important the past we shared had become for my relationship with Lena. Our common experiences in Kazakhstan had separated us even from our friends in Heidelberg, who had all been Holocaust survivors. Here, in America, there was not a person in millions who could relate to the path we had been forced to take. The further we traveled from our cottage in Ili, the more firmly that unique story bonded us together, for it seemed that only the two of us could know and understand what we had been through.

Yet, Lena was not particularly easy to live with as a wife or mother. When we had married, she had been an organizer and teacher in a school for young children and she fitted that role perfectly. She always acted like a school principal who feels responsible for the proper conduct of all those in her care, even more than for their scholarly progress. She had strict ideas about what constitutes proper behavior and was, as Steven put it, concerned above all that no one "disgrace" the family's reputation by wrong conduct.

Although no one ever did, Lena's vigilance was not easy to take for our children, especially Arthur, who was more exposed to it than Steven and so resented it more. But Steven was by no means exempt from her eager efforts to instill in our children the sense of propriety, not only to learn and behave well, but also to be clean and well groomed. (Lena's ministrations along this line extended for some time to me, too, with less success).

I was hardly aware at the time of the effect of Lena's character traits and foibles on our children. There were several reasons for this. Lena and I were always very close, not just because we truly loved each other but also because of the history we shared. I recalled with dread the time of her nervous illness in Cambridge and felt guilty for taking her there. Her recovery and good health were clearly a prerequisite for the happiness of all of us. Therefore, I wished to avoid anything that might disturb her, and hence found no faults.

Lena was proud of her old Jewish family as well as her proper Polish education (which she acquired with much less than the full approval of her father). She did everything possible to help my academic career, both in Germany and the United States. Although sometimes rigid in her zeal to promote good conduct, she demonstrated considerable flexibility in her personal behavior under very difficult wartime circumstances. She moved from Poland to Russia and Kazakhstan, then back and finally to Germany and America. On the way, she learned the necessary languages and skills to adjust to these very different environments. She managed to do well for herself, and still do the most in raising the children.

She was excellent at family matters including financial management. She was efficient, liked both shopping and bargains (one of my least favorite activities), and enjoyed travel and entertainment in moderation. Although she liked to reminisce about her family as wealthy landowners in Poland, almost as Jewish nobility, she had no taste, indeed no tolerance, for any extravagance. She valued learning but did not measure its worth by its cost. It was enough for Steven and Arthur to do well at the University of Michigan—it did not have to be Harvard. (She herself found time to graduate from college in history at Chicago's Roosevelt University).

Considering all this, it is not surprising that Lena, deep down, was herself much more interested in the future than in the past. After choosing to go to America, what she wanted most was for her family to settle, live, and work successfully in the new world, that is, to prosper as Americans. Accordingly, she approved of a far-reaching assimilation, although probably underestimating its eventual extent.

For more than a decade after we landed in New York City, it had been very easy for me to feel wholeheartedly enthusiastic about my new country. My first real challenge came in the late 1960s. The Vietnam War could not be ignored. It was to me not only an unnecessary conflict, but also particularly an American failure of policy and outlook: looking at the world as if it all is America and ignoring what isn't. The past matters less here somehow, while the future matters more, and the link between the two gets ignored. Knowing the history of the Vietnamese—their battles against the Japanese and French—it was totally naïve to expect an easy victory. But the American policymakers didn't seem to pay any attention to history; instead they based their plans solely on their confidence that everyone in the world would want to emulate Americans. I personally cared a great deal about history, for I knew that it shapes the future.

Vietnam was a moral disaster. We watched the death tolls climb on the nightly news and followed the rising anti-war movement at home. I was generally sympathetic to the protesters, though often not in favor of their tactics. At times it was alarming to see their activities escalating on campus. In the Business School our students tended to be more conservative, but as the decade progressed, some of them began to grow their hair long and wear outrageous outfits.

In 1968, a fateful year for Chicago and Vietnam, U.S. troops' massacre of the population of My Lai and North Vietnam's Tet Offensive against Saigon and other cities in South Vietnam, showed just how powerful our enemy had become. The number of U.S. troops in Southeast Asia peaked at half a million, with no sign that the war would be won or could be made winnable. Another election was approaching and mass demonstrations against the war and draft erupted in many U.S. cities and university campuses, from the East Coast to the Midwest and California. Dr. Martin Luther King and Robert F. Kennedy were shot. The Democratic National Convention was set for Chicago in October 1968. Mayor Daley instituted martial law and began fortifying the city in preparation for the expected demonstrations.

Downtown, the protesters and police battled for several nights. Chicago was in turmoil with the hippie demonstrators in action all over Grant Park on the beautiful lakefront. In the evening, we watched on TV how the Chicago cops wielded clubs and tear gas against the marchers.

Besides moral questions, I had a personal stake in the outcome. Steven was eligible for the draft. He had graduated at seventeen from the University of Chicago Laboratory School and attended college at the University of Wisconsin in Madison during 1963–1967. In the fall of 1967, he had started his first year at the University of Michigan Law School. The national draft lottery was held in 1969 in Washington, DC, in which he drew the number 202. This was close but lucky, as the highest number that was included in the draft was 195. By that time, he had taken a break from law school, and was teaching at the Vincennes Upper Grade Center, in an all-black neighborhood west of Hyde Park. This was classified as high-risk work and earned him a draft exemption.

At the University of Chicago, students occupied the administration building. Provost Edward Levi vacated his offices and waited the students out until they tired of occupying an empty building and left. The future U.S. Attorney General thereby avoided more drastic methods, such as inviting the local police, which would have meant a confrontation with the students. The faculty, generally frustrated by the noisy demonstrations and disruptions of class work, was itself deeply divided about the government's policies, the war, and how to proceed nationally and locally. There were heated debates and fractious and unpleasant meetings. The opponents of the war were increasingly numerous and vocal, the proponents increasingly uncertain and sullen.

I found myself occupying a middle ground. I was against the war, and therefore unwelcome among my more conservative colleagues. But my love of this country and my sincere desire to support our side made it impossible for me to indulge in the blanket attacks on the United States that the more radical professors expected of someone who was truly anti-war. I recall conversations with friends. We were walking through campus and arguing. Thanks to Vietnam, there were differences of opinion that we hadn't had before. It left me with an uneasy feeling; I was dissatisfied with my colleagues and with myself. For the first time, I was in a serious conflict with my adopted country.

Again, though I had seen this type of strife before, much worse was yet to come. During the 1930s I had watched fascist and leftist students battle it out on the streets of Kraków. Then, too, I had faced the uneasy feeling of being torn about my country. A patriotic Pole to that point, I had lost much of my affection for my homeland during those days when I saw the anti-Semitic elements gaining the upper hand.

At the time, many radical observers had drawn ominous comparisons between the 1930s and 1960s, but as an economist I knew they would never stand up. The disorders of the 1930s were caused by the unprecedented hardships caused by the Great Depression, and so much more—the economic world order—had been at stake. In the 1960s, despite some sluggish inflation at times, the economy was generally robust. So, if on the surface the disorderly scenes in the streets were the same in two eras, the underpinning motivations were wholly different.

The 1970s were the worst post–World War II decade in terms of high inflation, recession, and unemployment. Still, most of the time most American families earned enough income to prosper, and this included my family. After living for almost fifteen years in the apartment building on Blackstone Avenue and 58th Street, in Hyde Park, we had an opportunity to buy our third-floor apartment because the building was being converted into a condominium. We had become very used to the place and liked its excellent location near the university, good neighbors, and pleasant surroundings. All the tenants were planning to buy their own apartments to stay. We did not want to move either, but Lena had a better idea. She proposed to purchase the vacant lot next to our building, between our apartment building and the next building over to the north on Blackstone, and build a house there. That would give us more ground floor space and replace the old with the new one.

We got the building permit from City Hall and borrowed most of the money needed to fund the mortgage and equity on our house. What we didn't get from the bank, we borrowed from Lena's brother, Sam, who did well as a businessman in Brooklyn. We hired Bill Keck, one of two brothers whose architectural firm was locally well known and respected for contemporary design. Keck & Keck had designed the 1933 glass and steel "House of Tomorrow." At that time, Bill Keck had already enjoyed a long career—he was in his mid-sixties. He planned a two-story, three-bedroom house of glass and red brick, with large windows and an attractive sloped roof. It would fit in well with the older brick buildings in that historical neighborhood. Owning your own home is an important part of "the American dream."

The "ownership society" that politicians now talk about in the first decade of the twenty-first century is an old concept. Erich Preiser, my old Heidelberg professor, advocated a more equitable, broad-based distribution not only of income but also of wealth. He believed that this was highly desirable for a well-functioning market economy and a democratic sociopolitical system, as it would help expand social fairness and individual liberty. Citizens with more at stake may make better and more responsible economic and political decisions.

One of my earliest studies of the cyclical indicators that aid in predicting economic trends had been expanded into *Orders, Production, and Investment*, and the book was published by Columbia University Press in 1973. Here, I assembled data going back to 1870 to study relations between new and unfilled orders, production, shipments, and inventories. Another by-product from this analysis was one of the NBER's shorter "Occasional Papers" entitled "Unfilled Orders, Price Changes, and Business Fluctuations." In this paper, I explained the movements in the price level caused by changes in excess demand (as measured by changes in unfulfilled orders). This was a cutting-edge study with potential implications for economic policy. It caught the attention of the Moscow Institute of Economic and International Relations. They invited me to make a professional visit to the Soviet Union. As I contemplated a return to Russia, suddenly the old days didn't seem so distant anymore.

The economists who invited me could have had no idea that I had spent time in the Gulag, but when the granting of my visa was delayed for several months—from late spring to early fall of 1974—I began to wonder if some scrupulous apparatchiks in the KGB (Soviet Committee for State Security) had perhaps found out the truth. Finally, my papers arrived. The Soviets paid for my ticket. I flew from Chicago via London, landing at Moscow's Sheremetyevo Airport. When I arrived, my suspicions were confirmed. The delegation of economists who had come to meet me held aloft a sign with the name Zharnovits, the same correct Russian spelling that Stalin's NKVD (People's Commissariat for Internal Affairs) agents had used for me thirty-five years earlier (not my current Zarnowitz spelling).

How things had changed. Then I had ridden across Russia in a crowded cattle car, with a hole in the floor serving as the only bathroom for fifty people. Now, I was being greeted in the Soviet capital by a delegation of leading scientists. Soon we were speeding toward the city in a black limousine. For me, it was a personal triumph.

While I was in Moscow, the limousine was under my command and I took advantage of this opportunity, seeing the sights of this vital, but rather dreary city. I made my presentation in English and my speech was warmly received. I stayed in the Academy of Science building, which was obviously the kind of place where one's conversations were very likely to be overheard. As a result, Russian economists I met were always tight-lipped when we were indoors. But this gave way to a welcome change as soon as we were in the streets, enjoying the warm autumn air.

We talked freely in Russian. I was surprised at their degree of honesty about economic matters. They informed me that, frankly, they had no faith in their own government's statistics. Therefore, they were forced to view business cycle work as an abstract exercise rather than a practical one. What use was it to make predictions based on phony numbers? It also became clear through our conversations that they did not put too much faith in the American government's numbers, either.

There was much professional intensity, interest, and friendliness in our exchanges. I went to some shops, bookstores, and restaurants, even made

both agreed that he had done the right thing. But, during the late 1960s and the 1970s, inflation in the United States increased from entirely tolerable (about 2 percent) to high (14 percent) levels. At the same time, and contrary to the then prevailing economic theory, the unemployment rate also rose sharply, from about 4 to almost 10 percent. The unfortunate combination was given the ill-fitting label "stagflation" and depressed American morale, and the image of the U.S. economy.

The Ford (1974–1976) and Carter (1976–1980) years were character-ized by high oil prices, high inflation, and generally much dissatisfaction with, and anxiety about, the economy. The slowdown—and recession se-quence in 1973–1974 was influenced by unusual cost–and price hikes and supply restrictions. Oil politics became front-page news. An oil embargo from the Organization of Petroleum-Exporting Countries (OPEC) led to long lines at gas stations around the country. The Middle East, which was to be the most vulnerable area for foreign policy in the late twentieth and early twenty-first century, was beginning to show its importance.

This conflict was beginning its modern phase in the 1970s. At the end of the decade, on November 3, 1979, I was celebrating my sixtieth birthday with a large and joyous party in Chicago, when the news arrived that ninety people, most of them Americans, had been taken hostage at the U.S. embassy in Teheran, Iran, by students, who followed Ayatollah Khomeini, and demanded the return of the former Shah, then undergoing medical treatment in New York. It was the beginning of a new era.

Peaks and Valleys

10 ▪ ▪ ▪ While long intrigued by the mysterious relations of men with God, I only began to comprehend these difficult issues as I got older. I dislike organized religion (Voltaire's critique of it is one of the few points on which I agree with him). I like to pray alone, while in the Jewish religion prayer is supposed to be a communal activity. My discovery of both ancestral origins and faith came late in life.

In 1977, when we were in our late fifties, Lena and I made our first visit to Israel. From an economics meeting in Munich, we traveled by train to Venice for a few fine days. We then boarded a small Greek ship from the Adriatic port of Mestre for the Isthmus of Corinth and the city of Haifa. By the morning of the next day, we were passing through the tranquil sea near Bari, a port on the northern rim of the boot of Italy. It was sunny and mild throughout the several days and nights of our voyage, which was all enjoyable, especially in the evenings where the young returning tourists sang engaging Israeli songs.

We arrived in time before the Sabbath and checked into our small hotel high on Mt. Carmel, with a fine view of the bay. The next day we visited Fanny and Natek Wiener, who greeted us warmly. We saw the Bahai temple in the park on the slope of Mt. Carmel (Haifa is the headquarters of that religion, which recognizes Moses, Jesus, and other Jewish and Christian prophets). It felt like a familiar place because it recalled the similar temple in Wilmette, a northern suburb of Chicago.

From Haifa, we took the train along the sea south to Herzliyah, a tree-lined and handsome neighborhood, where we stayed briefly in a tower-like modern hotel before moving south to Tel-Aviv, Israel's capital of commerce and entertainment. We felt comfortable there, in our first large Jewish city. To Lena, it must have been a little like Warsaw of old. I gave a well-received lecture on business cycles and indicators. We attended a concert at the Mann Auditorium, with Zubin Mehta conducting the Israel Philharmonic and with Isaac Stern playing both the Brahms and the Prokofiev violin concertos—a feast of great music!

We went by bus to Jerusalem to stay as guests of Hebrew University. I had another presentation and met several friends. We went together by car to Bethlehem and beyond, south along the western shore of the Dead Sea, where we floated in the salty water. We went up by the funicular railway to the famous rock of Massada where Jews, beleaguered by the Romans, committed mass suicide. We passed the sites of ancient Sodom and where the Dead Sea Scrolls were found. We moved to Hebron to visit the cave of the patriarchs and then returned to Jerusalem. In a separate trip by bus we went up north to Lake Tiberias and across the Galilee to the beautiful mountain town of Safed, a resort with many artists near Israel's northern border.

It was all a fabulous pilgrimage through the ancient Holy Land and modern Eretz (Land of) Israel, with many moments of enchantment (for example, on Mt. Carmel, Tiberias, and at Safed), of deep reflection (in the old city of Jerusalem), and sadness (in a cemetery in Ramat Gan where Lena's sister is buried—she went there when she was a young, ardent Zionist, married, and died in childbirth). At the Wailing Wall, I could not hold back tears thinking of the multitudes who had perished over the ages without ever making it "in the year to come" to Jerusalem. Along with so many others, I stuck a little piece of paper with a few words addressed to God between the stones.

If there is a place on earth where faith can indeed move the mountains, it is Israel, both new and ancient. After a little less than two thousand years in exile and dispersion, most of the time isolated, discriminated against or persecuted, Jews came back in large numbers to what became Palestine. They rebuilt a country, an army, and a language, and eventually won a war of independence and their own state. In accomplishing these feats against all odds, many were moved by secular ideas, others by religious belief, or sheer desperation. But it is hard to imagine how history could have taken such a turn without the powerful spiritual appeal of the return to the homeland of the Jewish people, this Promised Land as recorded in "the book."

As the Bible tells it, it was the Jewish people who, led by Moses, crossed the desert after the exodus from Egyptian bondage, received the Torah, ruled ancient Israel under their prophets and kings, and returned there after exile in Babylon. History, through the many voices of Clio, its muse, tells us that centuries later the Romans conquered Israel along with the entire far and wide Mediterranean world. But Christianity, originating in the same land and people, conquered Rome. Faith of this intensity does, indeed, move mountains.

Along with many other visitors to Israel, I had a sense of presence of the great spiritual power that seems to have predestined the history of this country. It is not a feeling common to many places, but then this is a rather special place in the way it evokes faith and imagination.

It is here, and especially in Jerusalem, where monotheism first really took roots and where God's transcendence may have been first fully recognized. This is where He has been proclaimed the Lord of all men and of all creation, thrice holy ("kaddosh," or later and elsewhere "sanctus"). This is where he who comes in our Lord's name is blessed ("barukh" or "benedictus"). I was overwhelmed by the grandeur of all that happened here in ancient times: in Hebron and Jerusalem, on the Temple Mount, the Via Dolorosa and Golgotha, in Galilee and Massada. Great religions arose together with complex systems of thought and ethics. Inspired works of art and music followed over the centuries.

But I was also horrified by the tragic elements in the long aftermath. Fierce conflicts arose among the once intimately related religions, creeds, and sects. Where love had been preached, intolerance, wars, and persecution now reigned supreme. Tyrants imposed religion by force. The times of great good alternated with times of greater misery depending on whether these rulers were benevolent or tyrannical, generous or narrow-minded. Could it be in the tiny land where Jews and Christians had their common origins, and where even Islam gained an important foothold six centuries later, that the seeds of all of this grandeur and horror were sown? The answer "yes" may sound incredible but it cannot be denied. Judaism and Christianity have altered the course of history decisively, through their own closeness and alienation, as well as through their interaction and conflict with the Greco-Roman world and later with Islam.

Great progress has been made in technology and basic and applied sciences during the last century. Who can doubt what is visible all around us? Scientific and technological progress is by no means automatic and assured—it requires thriving education, general and academic, especially in math and sciences. Beyond that, it needs breakthroughs, which may come from the sudden insights of inspired or lucky pioneers, or more typically, from long joint work by great minds. Some of the best scientists and inventors are unknown because their discovery or invention can only be attributed to a long series of almost anonymous team workers who "stand on the shoulders of giants."

To generalize, the public takes this kind of progress more or less for granted, particularly in already highly developed countries. The public sees in this a profitable occupation for the talented and energetic, and counts on discoveries to be forthcoming. Actually, innovations come in very uneven, sometimes very long waves, and their volatility may cause serious economic and social problems.

Spiritual and moral progress is far less certain and hence it is sought after and valued by many people of good will. Any improvement to the inner life promises to bring on better relations between races, tribes and religions, nations, and classes. A mass movement forward and upward of this kind calls for great leaders with strong persuasive powers, perhaps more charismatic prophets than gifted thinkers or strategists. Intuitively, this former group is even thinner than the latter and is more rarely activated. Good and strong character may well be still less common and more difficult to develop than a strong and active mind, well and successfully applied.

The hunger for a morally and spiritually better world, along with ad-miration and respect for those who fight for it, explain the overwhelming grief that resulted from the assassinations of Mahatma Gandhi (1948) and Martin Luther King (1968), and the praise the world gave to their cam-paigns for freedom and justice and against imperialism and racism. The most recent enormous outpouring of these emotions occurred worldwide on April 2, 2005, after Pope John Paul II died.

There would be much publicized official mourning for the Holy Father by the 1.1 billion Catholics around the globe. But this grief was far more than that. The mourners included probably millions of non-Catholics and even non-Christians and included Jews and Muslims, as well as other believers and nonbelievers. John Paul II was justly celebrated as a hero in the struggle for more love and justice in this world.

I felt close to him for years because, although we were clearly very different, there were also remarkable parallels. He was about my age (born May 18, 1920, even slightly younger) and from a nearby town, Wadowice, located about 40 km from Oświęcim, east and slightly south. He studied at the Jagellonian University in Kraków until the war, as I did. He had Jewish friends at home and in school, witnessed in helpless horror the Holocaust in Nazi-occupied Poland, and remembered it well always. I have also long admired the first Polish pope's major character traits and actions. He bravely resisted the Communist regime in Poland by example, encouragement, visits, speeches, backing Solidarity, and other nonviolent means. His contribution to the fall of the Soviet empire, along with powerful forces and personalities inside and outside the USSR (Union of Soviet Socialist Republics), is widely recognized (for example, by Mikhail Gorbachev, elected Secretary General of the Communist Party of the Soviet Union in 1986 and a 1990 Nobel Peace Prize winner).

Karol Wojtyła from Wadowice became the first pope to visit a synagogue or a mosque. He went to the Wailing Wall in Jerusalem and placed a prayer note in a crevice there following an ancient Jewish custom. He mourned and prayed at Auschwitz and at Yad-va-Shem in Jerusalem. He led the Vatican to recognize the state of Israel. Most importantly, he declared anti-Semitism to be a sin. According to John Paul II, Jews are the "older brothers" of Christians. I fervently hope and pray that these papal instructions will be heard and followed and will help to put an end to centuries of disdain and persecution.

But a heartfelt desire is not the same as a belief based on reason. Is genuine progress toward a broad agreement on, and acceptance of, higher moral values really possible, let alone probable? No one can be sure of the answer, which only the future can provide. Most likely, progress will be made but it will be very uneven over time and space, as it was in the past. No political program offers a reliable solution to these issues; all people of good can fall back only on faith, good works, and hope.

The 1980s, my last decade of teaching in Chicago, started from the troublesome peak in inflation, high interest rates, and an unusual sequence of two back-to-back recessions. But all this was due to past events, past policy errors, and the correspondingly harsh but necessary remedies. The latter included, first, tight money, and then, lower taxes, lower (less overvalued) dollar, and higher defense expenditures. These policies worked well and the economy improved better and more quickly than expected. Moreover, U.S. policy turned more successful, too: it got the credit for the fall of the Soviet empire, whatever are the true, more complex underlying sources.

So, after the political troubles of the Vietnam-dominated 1960s and the economic troubles of the inflation-dominated 1970s, the 1980s developed into a relatively tranquil and happy era. It was a good time to monitor events, teach what Chicago calls the "political economy," and discuss economic and political issues with students and faculty. These issues were always fiercely but intelligently debated on a campus that was unusual in providing strong representation to conservative as well as liberal ideas.

My family was flourishing. Arthur had finished the University of Chicago Lab School in 1976 and then attended college in Ann Arbor, with which he had become familiar during our visits to Steven there. He showed interest and growing talent in drawing, painting, and industrial design, and so decided to study in the school of art at the University of Michigan. He excelled at it and completed the school in 1976–1980. Both Lena and I (she particularly) worried about whether these interests were practical as a means of advancing Arthur's career. Fortunately, our doubts proved unfounded. In his last year there, Arthur had a successful exhibition of his artwork, which we proudly attended. (I later saw a painting by Arthur's hanging in the apartment of a friend who was a dean at the university.)

I had a sabbatical in 1980–1981 and we spent the academic year at Stanford University in Palo Alto. We traveled there in our trusted Buick. The National Bureau of Economic Research (NBER) had its western office there in a building scenically located on a wooded hill where deer would come close to my office for a visit. I had abundant time to do research, read, write, and study. I had friends and colleagues there from the NBER and the Hoover Institution: Robert Hall, Milton Friedman, Victor Fuchs, and others. It was a productive and happy time.

Arthur, who had just graduated, joined us on this trip and stay, which turned out to be very fortunate. For nearly a year, until Lena and I returned to Chicago, he lived with us and found a job as an engineer and industrial designer. He found that he enjoyed the work and remained in California to live and work in a succession of larger companies. In time, he became proficient and highly regarded for computer design of new products. His work was featured in some annual design issues of *Business Week*. Most importantly, he started dating Sally, the very talented and attractive youngest daughter of a family that had lived in California for generations. Sally went to college at Berkeley and completed her studies in architecture at Harvard.

They were married on September 14, 1986 at the home of her parents in Menlo Park, next to Stanford. It was a beautiful wedding on the big, grassy, and tree-lined lawn behind their house. Her extended family, neighbors, and friends were all there. A rabbi officiated and a string quartet provided the music. I danced a lot with Lena and Sally's mother, and we all, including Steven and his family, had a great time. Some Stanford faculty was among the guests as well as many friends of the bride and the groom (for example, George P. Schultz was teaching at Stanford at the time and his son also attended).

Parents often feel at a loss when children leave them to follow their own careers and establish their own families. But this departure is inevitable, a natural rhythm of family life. Moreover, the parents are frequently more than compensated by the arrival of their grandchildren. All of this happened in our case and was clear to Lena and me.

We returned to Chicago after a year at Stanford, but my time there was running out. Everyone on the Chicago faculty, including the best known senior professors, were expected to formally retire at the age of seventy, even though some may have taken the option to continue to teach for a time. In November 1989, my time had come.

A traditional ceremony was held at the faculty's Quadrangle Club, an event that went well in the opinions of those attendees we heard from. I was proud of the speakers (presumably self selected) that included my distinguished colleagues George Stigler and Arnold Zellner. Stigler, a prominent theoretical and empirical microeconomist, was mildly congratulatory while still exhibiting his well-known, even feared, sharp wit and critical sense. He razzed me for my bent toward empiricism and accused me of showing insufficient respect for, and service to, theory. So, this debate had followed me from my dissertation to my retirement party. Zellner, likewise a world-class scientist, best known for work in Bayesian statistics and econometrics, offered an interesting selective assessment of my contributions. We then ate and drank, and had a good time reminiscing until late at night.

Retirement for me would not be the usual affair of Florida golf courses and leisure. My time at Chicago's Graduate School of Business had been the most important period of my career, but I was not finished. At 70, I was still eager and ready for work. And new opportunities soon presented themselves. The Soviet disintegration led to changes in Central and Eastern Europe. American economists were in high demand. Vaclaw Klaus, a conservative Czech economist and monetarist follower of Milton Friedman, visited Chicago and spent some time with the faculty and students at both the Department of Economics and the Graduate School of Business. He later became Czechoslovakia's prime minister. Our dean and faculty helped to establish and staff the first American School of Business in Prague. I spent a semester there in the early 1990s teaching macroeconomics.

Prague is a city of a great past and rare beauty. It reminded me of Kraków, but it is larger and still more impressive, with a particularly beautiful river and bridges with towers and statuary. The Vltava or Moldau is immortalized in Smetana's musical paean to the Czech homeland "Ma Vlast." For those of us who had dollars, prices were very low but were adjusting upward slowly in the new markets. The Hradčany castle on the hill enriches the views of Prague much like the Wawel castle on the hill does in Kraków. I walked a lot and admired the variety of sights and neighborhoods of the city surrounded by beautiful woods. The old Jewish quarter with its famous synagogue and cemetery deserves a special note. Rabbi Loew, who is said to have invented the Golem in the sixteenth century, may be buried there.

The opera house, near the older one where Mozart's *Le Nozze di Figaro* and *Don Giovanni* had their first popular triumphs, had me enthralled. A ticket cost less than a movie did in Chicago. I saw several good and not-so-good performances (a *Madama Butterfly* with an excellent Polish soprano and *Abduction from the Seraglio* sung in Czech!) as well as some first-rate concerts.

Along with other visiting professors from the United States, I lived in a dormitory not too far away and commuted to work by streetcar. I taught macroeconomics, which turned out to be new, somewhat strange, and difficult for my students whose practical experience had been limited to a Soviet-style planned economy. They were eager to learn and reminded me of myself, when I had just arrived at Heidelberg and had to quickly catch up with a huge body of new economic thought.

They were most interested in the merits and demerits of the market system, which had been portrayed very negatively under the Soviets. They had heard a lot of bad stuff about it and my counterweight to that was welcome. The whole debate was important. They were eager to embrace a free market in a cautious way. They wanted economic growth but did not want the inequities that inevitably go with the market system. Our talks spilled out of the classrooms. Very often, we continued our arguments at bars and restaurants over a cold glass of excellent Czech beer.

I returned to Chicago from Prague in December 1991. Then, after about a year, the dean of our school asked me to help again and make a shorter visit to the newly independent Ukraine. Viktor Yushchenko, at that time president of the central bank, had asked for help in fighting rapidly rising inflation. I was to be joined by a young Italian expert on inflation who had recently assumed a faculty position in Chicago. This was too interesting an opportunity to miss, so I accepted, with Lena's consent, and made the trip in three weeks.

Kiev seemed more isolated from the west than Moscow and very much in need of closer economic and political ties. There was much internal infighting going on in a country long divided between the western part, Ukrainian in language and national sentiment, and the eastern part, which was Russian-speaking with strong pro-Russian tendencies. It was soon clear that Yushchenko was a strong Ukrainian patriot and pro-western rather than pro-Russian. But he had to maneuver carefully to avoid alienating the important eastern faction in the parliament and the executive. The parliamentary leader was Leonid Kuchma who later, in July 1994, became the president of the Ukraine and who won this office again in 1999. Yet Kuchma was widely suspected of corruption and tended to use his powers autocratically and outside legal boundaries in order to hold on to his position.

Yushchenko was young and good looking. People that were close to him in the central bank half-jokingly called him "Sylvester," in order to compare him to the American actor Stallone. I recalled this a decade later, when fraud deprived him of the office of president, but he won it in the second election. This last election was better supervised and cleaner after big demonstrations showed him to be the real choice of the people. It was also big news that poison had been mixed into his food by his opponents, which ruined Yushchenko's handsome face and sent him to a hospital in the west.

Most importantly, at the time of my visit, Yushchenko was sufficiently curious and intelligent to learn from the experiences of other countries that inflation, a monetary phenomenon, required a properly timed and administered national monetary policy. Yushchenko heeded our advice and that of other experts and implemented monetary reforms that went far in alleviating his country's inflation problem. When we arrived in Kiev, the Ukrainian karbovanets was in accelerating decline not only relative to the U.S. dollar, which was the king in the currency exchanges that sprung up everywhere, but even relative to the Russian ruble. The money supply must have been rising swiftly, for inflation was rapid and approaching the hyperinflation that occurred in the past when a central bank financed continuing government deficits. In September 1996, following our visit, a new Ukrainian currency, the hryvna, was introduced. This broke the pace (or gallop) of the inflation. The hryvna settled at about U.S.$6.30.

Kiev (spelled Kiyev in Russian) is smaller than the two principal Russian cities and older, but no less interesting and attractive. It was severely damaged when it was taken by the Germans in World War II, but was completely rebuilt. I recall its famous buildings (the cathedral of St. Sofia, the monastery of Pecherskaya Łavra), monuments (that of the Cossack leader, Bohdan Khmelnytsky, no hero to his enemies and victims, Poles and Jews) and boulevards (the broad and colorful Kreshtshatik, flanked by green hills and red and yellow historic and office buildings). I prayed in a synagogue in Podol during the high holidays. This was a large Jewish district before the war and the Nazi devastation. I also prayed in the Babi Yar, a wooded area in the middle of the city, where a mass murder of Jews took place and where a monument in remembrance has been erected. In the train station, I saw a large group of orthodox Jews who were traveling to a small town in which a rabbi they admired was buried. I attended a performance of Verdi's "Nabucco" in the Shevchenko Theater of Opera and Ballet, a decent performance although hardly matching the standards of the Met or Italy. The choir was dressed in black and white robes, not unlike those of the praying Hassidim.

On my return from Kiev, I found an invitation from the Center of International Business Cycle Research (CIBCR), then an institute of Columbia University in New York, to join them. The director of CIBCR was Geoffrey H. Moore, my erstwhile boss and later colleague, friend, and coauthor, who had retired from the NBER. He appealed to me personally to work with him to revive the type of business cycle research no longer practiced at the Bureau and largely neglected or even opposed elsewhere.

It was a very attractive offer. Research in this area has been my lifetime work and remained important to me, as it had for Geoff. I knew that working with him and others in New York would likely prove more productive and enjoyable than working alone while retired in Chicago. I made a short trip to New York to confer with friends, notably Dr. Marcel Tuchman, and my potential employers at CIBCR and Columbia. I found that my New York salary would be more than twice as large as my income in Chicago. Also, we could have a comfortable and inexpensive (rent-controlled) Columbia faculty apartment at 119th and Broadway. This was very close to the CIBCR office. I returned enthusiastic and ready to accept.

Lena had agreed with me for a long time in placing great value on work and its accomplishments. She was hardly opposed to my arguments about higher income and the tie with Columbia. But Lena was devoted to our home in Hyde Park and reluctant to leave it. I understood and sympathized with this, but gave more weight to the prospect of a more active and happier life in New York for me and therefore probably also for her. In the end, Lena agreed, but rather reluctantly. She also had strange suspicions about some of the people I was going to work with at the CIBCR, but may have dropped them as groundless.

Steven helped us to prepare for the move. He came to Chicago and we bought a sofa, chairs, and a fine new television set at Marshall Field for the living room. The furniture and the TV served us well and are still with me in New York. Steven also drove us to the airport.

Now, with the hindsight of knowing what awaited Lena and me, I sometimes cannot help but wonder if I was not too work-addicted and insufficiently attached to our family home. In other words, should we have stayed in Chicago instead? This is probably an irrational guilt feeling. After all, everybody agrees, no one falls ill because of a change in the place of living, whether it is Chicago, New York, or any other place. This is true, yet no solace, only mildly comforting.

Our apartment near Columbia and the CIBCR office at Uris Hall on the campus was a real bargain in New York. It was of good size and location, but it was only a rental and modest when compared with our own house in Chicago. We had a few good friends who visited us and went out for walks and to nearby restaurants on a few occasions. But Lena was not well, got tired quickly, and needed help. She liked working with domestics from foreign countries, particularly Poland. Fortunately, the city was full of women seeking this kind of work and with information about them in numerous publications. I still have an address book with many of their names and telephone numbers. We were generally well served and got along fine with their help, despite high turnover, which can be expected in the large and mobile city.

After a few months, Lena was thoroughly tested at nearby St. Luke's Hospital, where we learned the bad news that her Parkinson's disease was accelerating. It is a devastating illness that afflicts body and mind of a patient. The long suffering and decline of Lena was inevitably the cause of deep sorrow for our family. For me, the closest, it was a distress hard to bear. I suffered many losses of loved ones before—father, mother, grandmother, brother, to mention only the closest family—but none hit me in normal times and mature life and none felt so cruel. Even though recent and vivid in my memory, the events of Lena's sickness and passing are difficult for me to write about. I must keep the account brief and not err by dwelling on the personal tragedy.

Lena spent several years in a succession of hospitals and nursing homes, all providing good care but also depressing, not only to the visitors (surprisingly few) but also the still sensitive patients. The first of these was St. Luke's Hospital, where Lena eventually fell into coma for three weeks, during which she was unconscious and was fed intravenously. I was desperate and hoped every day for a miracle, but one young doctor told me she will get out of this, and so did my friend Maciek (Dr. Marcel Tuchman) on a visit. They were right and she improved temporarily.

Next stop after the hospital was the Amsterdam Nursing Homes on the avenue of the same name in Manhattan. Lena's room had windows looking across the avenue to the Cathedral of St. John the Divine. Ever since then, it was one of my favorite places to pray: it is a huge and never finished Gothic church open to all denominations and religions, with many statues and memorials including one to the Holocaust. I came each day and rejoiced when Lena greeted me or looked better.

We thought that Lena might better like the Jewish Hospital and Home for the Aged on 116th Street nearer to our apartment. But it was not much better and, not surprisingly, she did not want to be in any of the nursing homes. Meanwhile, CIBCR had lost the connection to and the use of the office space at Columbia. Similarly, I lost the use of the Columbia faculty apartment. CIBCR staff got divided, some choosing FIBER (Foundation for International Business and Economic Research), others ECRI (Economic Cycle Research Institute). Both organizations moved to new offices, both in midtown, on or near 42nd Street. I stayed with FIBER.

These changes and the very high costs of nursing homes in Manhattan forced me to consider moving Lena and myself to New Jersey, as close to the city and to work as possible. The Castle Hill nursing home in Union City, NJ, was reputed to be as good as any around. One of the FIBER investors had a home in which I lived in nearby Weehawken. The house was close to a bus stop to the Lincoln Tunnel and then to Times Square. Over a weekend, Steven helped both Lena and I to move.

I was still able to visit Lena at least once each day. It was usually in the morning, before taking the bus to work in Manhattan, but sometimes also in the evening, and always for longer times on the weekend. The nursing home was, indeed, good, but it may have also been a matter of an adjustment over time on Lena's part. She happened to be a little aggressive in the Jewish home and became either better adjusted or more resigned in Castle Hill.

Most but not all of the nursing home patients are old and frail and many are in poor mental as well as physical shape. It is this that makes these places so depressing. It might have been wishful thinking, but I thought at the time that Lena looked and behaved better than most and would be able to make friends.

But on June 6, 2000, in the morning, I got a call from Castle Hill that Lena had passed away during the night. I rushed over and found her laid out in the attic, and could only kiss her cold lips. The cause of death was listed as being "congestive heart failure, Parkinson's disease." With our sons, some family and a few friends present, Lena was buried in a Jewish cemetery on Long Island, New York. The gravestone erected above her coffin awaits mine as well when I am gone and has the names of both of us, and parents, engraved on it.

While in Jerusalem, she and I had visited the nearby valley of Hinnon, where in ancient times waste from the city was kept and burned. This place, because of refuse and fires, that were always lit to prevent plague, was given the name "Gehenna" or hell. Jews used the word to tell of their worst time. I thought that our Gehenna had come and had to be borne with Lena's illness and hospitalizations in the late 1990s. Yet Lena's death, while painful to all of us who loved her, must have been a release from suffering for her, because I do not believe that Parkinson's alone had deprived her of all capacity and will to live.

One loves a woman with whom one has lived for more than 50 years. Lena and I shared other ties, though. We had both lost the world of our childhoods. We had met in far Kazakhstan and had become each other's only family. While I was simply trying to survive, she had taken it upon herself to care for others. In the years of the war I had seen only selfishness and cruelty. Her dedication to the orphans in Ili had reawakened my belief in altruism and human kindness. After the peace, she had brought between forty and sixty of those children back to Poland. They had settled in Israel, and had lived full lives. Lena always thought of this as her greatest work.

Lena also gets the credit for urging me to write my most important book. It was right after my Prague trip that I put the finishing touch on *Business Cycles: Theory, History, Indicators and Forecasting*, which was published by the University of Chicago Press in 1992. It combined some older material with my more recent work and, taken together, represented a summary of the major achievements of my career. I believe that I have put to rest any doubt about the usefulness of leading indicators in dating recessions and recoveries of the past. Not surprisingly, their capacity to help predict future patterns of cyclical behavior is less well accepted, but in my view significant as well.

It is tempting to accept the hypothesis that recessions are caused by unpredictable but adversely effective and widely propagated shocks because forecasts of recessions are indeed rarely made, let alone timely and validated. Models that have gained substantial professional favor are nevertheless incapable of reproducing many past recessions, let alone predicting new ones. And it is impossible to match some recessions that have been well recognized and dated with equally well-identified and dated shocks.

So I disbelieve the "general equilibrium" models and "real business cycle" theories some find appealing and representative of "mainstream" economics. I cannot find in them general and persuasive arguments that business cycles of experience are due to the propagation by the market economy of randomly occurring outside or inside impulses. Nor do I know of any valid tests or evidence that support this idea. There is no doubt that shocks do occur and at times contribute to economic fluctuations, but this is far from being the whole story and will often not be even the main story. So I argue that more attention needs to be given to the old and new endogenous theories of business cycles, which can explain how economic forces can bring about recessions and recoveries. Shocks are still important but as an amplifying rather than a primary causal factor. My 1999 article "Theory and History Behind Business Cycles: Are the 1990's the Onset of a Golden Age?" (*Journal of Economic Perspectives*, Spring 1999) treats the issue extensively.

On June 27 and 28, 2003, a conference in my honor was held in Essen, Germany, under the title "Business Cycles: Theory, History, Indicators and Forecasting" (named after the book with the same title). The meeting was arranged by the Rheinisch-Westfälisches Institut (RWI) of Eisen and the Ifo-Institut of Munich. It was attended by a prominent group of European and U.S. economists, some of whom voiced substantial agreement with my point of view on business cycle theory and policy. In particular, Andrew Filardo from the Bank for International Settlements in Basel (who holds a Ph.D. from the University of Chicago, Department of Economics) presented a paper "The Enduring Core of Business Cycles," of which I thought highly. Several fine papers were offered, for instance, by Professor Zellner from Chicago, Dr. Robert McGuckin from The Conference Board, Drs. Inklaar and Jacobs from Groningen, and Professors Lahiri (State University of New York) and Klein (Penn State). There were opening addresses from RWI, Ifo, and CIRET representatives, my concluding remarks and thanks, and a pleasant dinner and opera (Giordano's *Andrea Chenier* performed in the beautiful Aalto Theater).

This was naturally a very rewarding occasion for me. The Federal Reserve of Boston had held a conference along similar lines in June

1998. The book of these proceedings was entitled *Beyond Shocks: What Causes Business Cycles*. The hypothesis offered by many modern macroeconomists, that "shock-movements in important economic variables that occur for reasons we do not understand" have "caused the Asian crisis, the recessions of the 1970s and 1980s, and even the Great Depression" was called "unsatisfying" (J.C. Fuhrer and S. Schuh, pp. 1–2). Samuelson cited my observations on improved cyclical performance in the United States during the past fifty years and attributed it to "changed policy ideology, away from *laissez faire* and toward counter-cyclical macro policy" (pp. 34–35).

Geoffrey H. Moore passed away in the year 2000 at the age of eighty-six. He was a pioneer in the field of business cycle analysis, indicators and forecasting, a close coworker, and a good friend. That he was no longer with us was not only a major loss for our profession but also a personal loss for me. I was eighty-one years old, well past retirement age. Financially, I had no need for employment. Yet, I felt there was still work to be done. Marcel Tuchman, my old friend from Heidelberg, is now my doctor in New York as well. He has this same feeling. We both keep regular working hours.

He and I are both motivated by our Holocaust experiences. We are ambitious to prove ourselves and succeed. He believes that the Holocaust generation works harder. I don't know if we work harder, but maybe we work better because we make an effort to compensate for what was lost in the war. Maybe we have tried to prove something to ourselves. Perhaps, we also want it known that we were able to overcome the effects of extreme and deadly discrimination; indeed, that we were able to flourish in America, in New York, which is considered a place where it's hard to succeed. Are we trying to convince ourselves that we have made the most of our good fortune? Are we trying to compensate for the loss of friends and family? I cannot tell.

In 2000, I received an invitation to join the Economics Program of The Conference Board, the world's oldest, largest, and best-known business membership and research organization. Founded in 1916, it has nearly 2,000 member companies employing over 23 million people in sixty countries. It is an independent, global, nonpartisan, and nonprofit organization. In 1996, The Conference Board assumed control of the U.S. leading and other cyclical indicators. They now wanted me to help them select and analyze indicators and composite indexes for other countries. I knew the organization well and had worked with it in the past. I started working there on April 1, 2000.

The Conference Board office is in a modern building on Third Avenue near 52nd Street. I found an apartment nearby, and every morning I wake up and walk about fifteen minutes to get to work. I'm usually at my desk by 9:30 A.M. and stay until after 5:00 P.M. I very much like my job and working with the others at TCB—mostly young people, certainly so relative to myself. I am old but do not feel old. This, I think, is due mainly to keeping busy and taking pleasure in making my life count: I still do work that is considered useful and well compensated.

My main task now is to advise TCB on the selection of indicators for a number of important countries, the construction from them of composite leading and coincident indexes, the use of these data in dating and forecasting business cycles and growth, and interpretation of the results. In addition to the United States, we regularly produce cyclical indicators and indexes for France, Germany, United Kingdom, Mexico, Australia, Spain, Japan, and South Korea.

Along with my colleagues at TCB, I have visited a great many countries to present and discuss our work and its implications. I have flown around the world to Tokyo, Seoul, Paris, and back to New York. On a separate occasion, I have traveled to London, Frankfurt, and Mexico City. Currently, TCB does much work on the rapidly growing Chinese economy and its neighbors, so I visited Beijing, Hong Kong, and Singapore (for important regional conferences). These trips, to old and new, large and excitingly diverse cities, were of as much interest as fun (think of the Great Wall of China, the Imperial Palace, and Park in Tokyo, the seafronts and markets everywhere). My two recent trips to Poland, already noted, combined economic conferences in Warsaw and Krynitsa, with private side trips to Łańcut, Kraków, and Oświęcim.

I continue to write frequently for the TCB monthly report *Business Cycle Indicators* and occasionally for professional economic journals. My articles address selected economic developments and issues of current interest, for example, what are the principal new features and the retained historical features of the latest recession and recovery? The journal articles are oriented toward the academic economist and are more technical, for example, how best to decompose important measures of total economic

Victor Delivering a presentation at The Conference Board.

activity such as gross domestic product (GDP) or The Conference Board's composite index of coincident indicators into trend, cyclical, and random (irregular) movements? Sometimes, my colleagues and associates are also my coauthors.

Economics has a reputation of being both important and difficult. Hence, there is much respect for economists presumed to be smart professionals who perform critical and therefore well-rewarded tasks for business and government. But respect need not convey sympathy. There are many who see business as governed by greed and government as the tool of business and the rich and who accordingly have little love for the economists who are part of this evil system.

These are widespread attitudes fostered either by personal adversity and dissatisfaction or by ideological alienation. The opponents of the "excesses" of capitalism may themselves be well-off or are at least middle class. These critics may often be misguided or tend to exaggerate, but are not always wrong. Although markets generally work well, and indeed better than government commands in running an economy, capitalism suffers from excesses of its own. A network of proper institutions and the rule of law are necessary to insure that the market system and corporate governance function appropriately, with minimum damage from fraud and corruption. Market regulation, where needed, must not be inadequate, biased, or excessive.

Good economists can help create and maintain the right conditions for business, government, and the economy to function. What is most needed is good economic growth without excessive inflation and indebtedness or cyclical instability. Free trade and high standards of living are desirable. Unfair income distributions and labor market conditions are not. But there are conflicts between the objectives of good monetary, fiscal, trade, and other government policies, which may cause difficult tradeoffs and compromises. Corporate policies face different but equally difficult problems. In order to be managed well, they all require good information, expertise and a sense of what is right and achievable.

Economists do think in terms of prices and costs, revenues and expenditures, that is to say, the self-interest of the unit they serve such as a household or a firm. This is understandable and right because the unit is best served when its self-interest is being protected and promoted. Even government agencies have self-interest, which should be moderate but cannot be ignored, for instance, they tend to compete for money within the budget to serve the public better. But self-interest should not be confused with greed. The pursuit of happiness, presumably in self-interest, is good. Greed is a personal vice in religious but not necessarily socioeconomic terms. Excessive greed may become asocial. Capitalism may generate excessive materialism but does not have to; the two are not same. Planned systems may generate as much materialism, even when poorer.

Economists, being human, have hearts and brains. They feel and think. They are not necessarily too greedy for themselves or others and do not only favor the rich or a specific group. They may be either liberal or conservative. They are generally in favor of more, not less, equity and fairness, but even more in favor of higher and more stable growth for the economy as a whole, since this benefits all.

In my view, it matters much more how good you are as an economist than whether you are liberal or conservative. Allegiance to political programs may warp your economic reasoning. I consider myself to be an independent and a classic liberal: all for personal liberty (but also personal responsibility), for all freedoms as FDR (Franklin Delano Roosevelt) listed them; and for the continued separation of powers and of the state from religion. But I am also for limited government in domestic and economic affairs, while strong on defense and security. I consider myself conservative on family and moral matters.

I have concentrated for a long time on the subject of business cycles and my dream as an economist is to be able to reduce cyclical instability and increase growth. The progress of research, knowledge, and technology together with certain structural changes have contributed to the achievement of these goals, which are happily related. I believe that higher growth and less cyclical instability go together. Further progress in economic research can yield additional advances in increasing economic growth and lessening the frequency and severity of business recessions and slowdowns. But it is important to work on improved ideas and models, test them repeatedly for different countries and periods, and avoid any assumptions that are untested and could well prove wrong. I hope that others realize that it is particularly important not to automatically follow models whose main attraction is that they happen to be popular at the time.

That is my dream as an economist.

Epilogue: An Octogenarian in a New Millennium

Lately, I get a recurring dream many times a month. I'm walking through a labyrinth of streets in an old town. Sometimes I even go through the rooms of strangers' apartments, but even then I continue walking. It's unpleasant but I have no choice. It's always the same motif of walking. The town could be Oświęcim, or another town in Poland. Sometimes it's the countryside and walking through the fields is easy. But whenever I need to open doors and pass through them I get a sensation of extreme frustration and anxiety. I believe this dream has something to do with overcoming obstacles. Somehow I'm destined to pass through these obstacles, and eventually I succeed. But who puts them up for me? I don't know.

Writing this memoir has made me think about the past. My children tell me I have a good, long-term memory, but they can't know, as I do, how much has been lost. I wish I had kept a diary. One thing is clear from my life story, clearer now than ever before. I have gradually lost one person after another. I know I'm not alone in this. Rationally, I realize that I'm not to blame. But it's easier said than felt. I do feel some inexplicable guilt. It's cumulative and it gets worse as I get older. First, my father had a heart attack when I was just ten-years-old. Then I said goodbye to my mother and grandmother on the second day of the war during 1939. In the frozen labor camps of Karelia I had to leave behind my brother, Tadek. Finally, late in life, my wife Lena also died.

I know that many of my losses have been compensated by the promise of the next generation. My older son, Steven, is a lawyer who manages a large local real estate company. He is married to Kathy and is the father of Katie. Arthur and his wife, Sally, now live in San Jose, California, where she works in the city's planning department, while Arthur designs wireless computer products for palmOne Corporation. Their two sons are Ray and Walter. Both are excellent students and very handsome boys. I think the older looks more like his mother, the younger more like his father and perhaps like myself when I was young.

I try to keep healthy by swimming regularly as well as walking. There is a pool in my building, which I normally use daily when in New York (and not oversleeping). I read a lot all my life, fiction and nonfiction, and still do. But my eyesight is not what it once was. I enjoy classical music, as I always have, and subscribe to the Metropolitan Opera and the New York Philharmonic. I occasionally go out to the theater, movies, and restaurants (mostly with the Tuchmans). I call my sons and relatives (Sam, Lena's brother, and his daughter Edna; Janka, daughter of my aunt Eda) and get calls from them. I abstain from any other leisure activities.

Given the vulnerability of people of my age to a variety of ills and troubles, I clearly should have no complaints at all, and have none. Not only is my health reasonably good, but I am independent and able to help persons close to me with gifts larger than ever. Hopefully, I also contribute to the common good by paying in a larger share of taxes.

Indeed, it is a good life and I can only wish for it to continue. However, I am also fully aware of the overriding fact and force of mortality. Sometimes I feel its inescapable burden hard to bear and recall Dylan Thomas (1952): "Do not go gentle into that good night. Old age should burn and rage at the close of day. Rage, rage against the dying of the light." But more often I reflect that it is not only futile but wrong to rebel against the physical and moral order of the world. Great thinkers and creators faced mortality serenely, and it is well to learn from them.

A real burden for me is loneliness. There is no way to prepare for the loss of the person closest to you for more than 50 years. None of the deep losses, of which I suffered so many as a child and young man, provided any parallels or guidance to me in my latest predicament. I am even lonelier now than I was in the war, though then I was just as alone. The difference was that then I saw it happening to other people all around me. I was part of a vast experience of loss. Now it is a solitary experience.

People of strong religious faith in an afterlife have a ready source of spiritual relief from the common exposure of being bereft of a loved person. Friends who have such faith told me in a matter-of-fact tone not to grieve because I will soon be reunited with Lena in paradise. I felt a deep desire to share the same belief, despite being more of an intellectual than a religious person (or perhaps precisely because of that). While seeing no purely rational argument or persuasive evidence that would resolve all doubts on that score, I also understand and favor Pascal's bet in favor of the existence of the afterlife rather than against it.

To the younger generations my story might seem exceptional, but I know from experience how many others went through the same trials that I did. So, I don't like to claim too much. Instead, I will attempt to impart some lessons learned in a long lifetime.

I value faith and the good it can do for people's character and behavior. But I am also skeptical and distrustful of organized religion, which tends to become self-centered, orthodox, and hostile to outsiders who are considered nonbelievers. Now there are new risks posed by bodies of the doctrinaire when Islamist terrorists attack targets in America and Europe with their suicide bombs and when strong political and military responses come from governments influenced by religious constituencies. While I believe that a determined and effective war on terror is needed and justified, I hope it never degenerates into a new religious war or crusade.

Many of my friends and relatives believe that the U.S. government misled the country into the war in Iraq. I don't believe this has been fully demonstrated, but I agree that the conflict has been mishandled.

All wars are horrors but not all are errors. Some must be fought and won for a just cause. World War II, most horrible as it was, is probably the best example—it had to be won to save the world from a new barbarism, legitimized slavery, tyranny, and atrocities.

Most people do want more peace and justice in the world, and many will work, fight, and sacrifice for these goals. Among them are individuals of great powers and talents and a mass of less exceptional civilian and military personnel. I hope and believe that these efforts will produce more social, political, and economic progress over time, and perhaps even some moral improvements.

This is as much optimism as I can muster, and may be realistic only because it relates to social justice, not neighborly love, and because it leaves open some of the most important questions. Yes, progress is likely to come, but how broad, fast, and strong will it be? Still, my expectations are clearly much more modest than the highest, religiously inspired ideal of the universal reign of love, which, I am afraid, is rather utopian.

To be just and fair are good character traits that are not uncommon and norms of behavior to which people of good will generally manage to adhere to. To love your neighbor as yourself is far more demanding and difficult. Many are not lovable and many do not even love themselves. Charity as a commandment calls for man to practice a divine virtue for which he may not be naturally equipped. To call for charity as a requirement of universal progress can be a sincere expression of a high ideal that has little to do with the realities of the day. When the ideal is voiced by the insincere for political ends, it is just pure hypocrisy.

I have always been a survivor. Though I was not in a concentration camp, I am a member of the Holocaust generation. As such, I have worked hard and tried to be a good person. I never felt like I had to somehow compensate for the great loss of my peers, but I have strived to be worthy of their memory. It is a source of pleasure to me to have done well after the years, and also to have seen that my contemporaries from Heidelberg have succeeded. As they say in America, "we made a difference." Despite our losses we reasserted ourselves and accomplished something. I lost my father too early to have really learned to know him as a person, but I hope that he would have been proud of me.

I now think there are more important things than success. I think that character is more important than intellect, and more rare. It's very difficult to combine both and do well, and the world doesn't make it any easier.

Acknowledgments

Last but not least? This section is much more than that. Its conventional title does not do justice to its importance. Without the help of my family and personal friends, this memoir could not have been written, and without the help of my business associates, it could not have been published. The thanks that follow are heartfelt.

Lapses of memory threaten the accuracy, and delusions of memory threaten the reliability, of memoirs. My sons, Steven and Arthur, helped me to avoid and reduce these risks. So did Jean Goetz (Janka Kupperman, daughter of Sam Engelman, my wife's brother).

Of my colleagues at The Conference Board, Gail Fosler, President, has done most to promote this book—as well as helping me to continue work on business cycles and indicators at TCB; she has my deep gratitude and admiration. I would also like to thank Thai Jones for his help in bringing the manuscript to fruition.

In the Communications Department at TCB, Director Frank Tortorici and Manager Carol Courter paved the way for the book to be edited and published by Praeger Publishers. Marino Belich, formerly staff photographer at The Conference Board, helped me to select and arrange the photos. Clyde Conway provided help with the map of Poland.

Notes

CHAPTER 1

1. Lanzut Societies, *Lanzut: The Life and Destruction of a Jewish Community*, pp. XVII–XVX.

2. Ibid., p. XXV.

3. "A Polish Anniversary," *The New York Times*, May 2, 1888.

4. Potocki, *Master of Łańcut*, p. 64.

5. "Poland Left a Wreck by War," *Boston Daily Globe*, July 3, 1915.

6. Potocki, *Master of Łańcut*, p. 64.

7. "Harvests Below 1928 in Central Europe," *The New York Times*, Sept. 16, 1929.

CHAPTER 2

1. Dwork, Debórah, and Robert Jan van Pelt. *Auschwitz: 1270 to the Present.* W.W. Norton and Company, 1996, p. 56.

2. "Poland Is Gripped by Economic Crisis," *The New York Times*, Jan. 25, 1931.

3. "Recovery Program Outlined in Poland," *The New York Times*, Oct. 26, 1935.

4. "Polish Budget Is Passed," *The New York Times*, Feb. 14, 1932.

5. "The Jews in Poland," *The Living Age*, Feb. 1937.

6. Wolnerman, Ch., A. Burstin, M.S. Geshuri (Editors), *Oświęcim; Auschwitz Memorial Book.* Oshpitsin Society. 1977. Reference is in section entitled, "Oshpitzin as Reflected in Various Journals," page number unknown. For clarity's sake, I have changed Oshpitzin (which I believe is Hebrew for Oświęcim) to Oświęcim in the text.

7. Ibid., p. 155.

8. "The Jews in Poland," *The Living Age*, Feb. 1937.

9. Wolnerman et al., *Oświęcim; Auschwitz Memorial Book*, p. 147, for the description of the view from the Soła.

10. "Duke Shows Guests Model Vienna Homes," *The New York Times*, Feb. 12, 1937.

11. "Europe Today," *Washington Post*, July 6, 1937.

12. "Student Riots Close Cracow University," *The New York Times*, Nov. 16, 1929.

13. Jan Kott, in conversation with Allen J. Kuharski. "Raised and Written in Contradictions: The Final Interview." p. 104.

14. Quoted in "The Jews in Poland," *The Living Age*, Feb. 1937.

CHAPTER 3

1. Wegierski, Dominik, *September 1939*. Minerva Publishing Co., 1940. The description of the feelings in Kraków in the week before the war comes from p. 12.

2. "Warsaw as It Was; Impressions of an August Visit," *Times of London*, Sept. 20, 1939.

3. Wegierski, *September 1939*, pp. 21–22.

4. Ibid., pp. 14 and 22.

5. Ibid., p. 74.

6. Ibid., p. 32.

7. Oświęcim Memorial Book. "I Wandered Like a Lost Sheep" by Ze'ev Peltzman, p. 489. Two Jewish youths were killed in the bombing of Oświęcim on that first day: Zushke Enger and David Schnitzer.

8. Bethell, Nicholas. *The War Hitler Won: The Fall of Poland, September 1939*. Holt, Rinehart and Winston, 1972. Both of these quotes are on p. 32.

9. Ibid., p. 1.

10. Ibid., p. 31. The author makes the point about the heavy burden of military expense on the Polish state.

11. Wegierski, *September 1939*, p. 28.

12. Bethell, *The War Hitler Won: The Fall of Poland, September 1939*, p. 27.

13. Wegierski, *September 1939*.

14. Ibid., p. 77.

15. Ibid., p. 49.

16. Ibid., p. 68.

17. "Poles Unprepared for Blow So Hard," *The New York Times*, Sept. 12, 1939.

18. "Devastation in Poland," *The Times of London*, Sept. 14, 1939.

19. Bethell, *The War Hitler Won: The Fall of Poland, September 1939*, p. 158.

20. Ibid., pp. 99–100.

21. Wegierski, *September 1939*, p. 64

22. "Ruins Mark Line of Nazi Advance," *The New York Times*, Sept. 15, 1939.

23. "Germans Rout Foe; France Admits There Is No Longer Any Front as Poles Withdraw," *The New York Times*, Sept. 15, 1939.

24. Bethell, *The War Hitler Won: The Fall of Poland, September 1939*, p. 136.

25. Wegierski, *September 1939*, p. 74.

26. Bethell, *The War Hitler Won: The Fall of Poland, September 1939*, p. 135.

27. "Capital Battered; Germans Subject It to an All-Day Shelling and Continuous Air Raids," *The New York Times*, Sept. 11, 1939.

28. "Polish Resistance Firm in 2 Battles," *The New York Times*, Sept. 16, 1939.

29. Bethell, *The War Hitler Won: The Fall of Poland, September 1939*, pp. 137–138.

30. "Flight Out of Poland," *The Times of London*, Sept. 20, 1939.

31. "Soviet Push Swift," *The New York Times*, Sept. 18, 1939.

32. "Flight Out of Poland," *The Times of London*, Sept. 20, 1939.

33. "Moscow Outlines Polish Partition," *The New York Times*, Sept. 19, 1939.

CHAPTER 4

1. Honig, Samuel, *From Poland to Russia and Back, 1939–1946: Surviving the Holocaust in the Soviet Union*. Black Moss Press, 1996, p. 59.

2. Ibid., p. 59.

3. "Western Ukraine Votes Soviet Rule," *The New York Times*, Oct. 28, 1939.

4. "Soviet Restores Service," *The New York Times*, Nov. 24, 1939.

5. Honig, *From Poland to Russia and Back, 1939–1946: Surviving the Holocaust in the Soviet Union*, p. 67.

6. "East Poland Reported Starving Because Russia is Taking Food," *The New York Times*, April 15, 1940.

7. Honig, *From Poland to Russia and Back, 1939–1946: Surviving the Holocaust in the Soviet Union*, p. 77.

8. Ibid., p. 78.

9. In Russian, this is said: *Glavnoe Upravlenie Lagerei*.

10. Gregory Paul R., and Valery Lazarev, eds. *The Economics of Forced Labor: The Soviet Gulag*. Hoover Institution Press, 2003; Foreword, p. x.

11. Honig, *From Poland to Russia and Back, 1939–1946: Surviving the Holocaust in the Soviet Union*, p. 92.

12. "Finland's Voice in the Symphonies of Jean Sibelius," *Current Opinion*, August 1914.

13. Gregory, *The Economics of Forced Labor: The Soviet Gulag*, p. 9.

14. Honig, *From Poland to Russia and Back, 1939–1946: Surviving the Holocaust in the Soviet Union*, p. 98.

15. Ibid., p. 94

16. Gregory, *The Economics of Forced Labor: The Soviet Gulag*; Foreword, p. x.

17. Honig, *From Poland to Russia and Back, 1939–1946: Surviving the Holocaust in the Soviet Union*, p. 119.

18. "German Thrusts Repelled," *The New York Times*, Nov. 17, 1941.

19. "Soviet Rail Line Built on Ice," *The New York Times*, Jan. 24, 1942.

CHAPTER 5

1. Description of the "Road of Life," is from Salisbury, Harrison. *The 900 Days: The Siege of Leningrad.* Harper & Row, 1969, pp. 393–422.

2. "Fifty Below Zero," *The New York Times,* Jan. 11, 1942.

3. Davies, Raymond Arthur, and Andrew J. Steiger, *Soviet Asia: Democracy's First Line of Defense.* The Dial Press, 1942, p. 105.

4. Davies, Norman, and Antony Polonsky (Editors), *Jews in Eastern Poland and the USSR, 1939–46.* St. Martin's Press, 1991, p. 148.

5. "Moscow Men for Kazakhstan," *Times of London,* Feb. 12, 1954.

6. Davies, *Jews in Eastern Poland and the USSR,* pp. 145, 158.

7. "Polish Army in Russia," *Times of London,* Jan. 10, 1942.

8. Davies, *Jews in Eastern Poland and the USSR,* pp. 154–155.

9. Ibid., p. 153.

10. Quoted in R. Davies, pp. 113–114. From N.N. Baransky's *Physical Geography of the U.S.S.R,* (Moscow, 1938).

11. Davies, *Soviet Asia: Democracy's First Line of Defense,* p. 110.

12. "Among the Kazakhs," *Times of London,* Feb. 25, 1953.

13. Davies, *Soviet Asia: Democracy's First Line of Defense,* p. 117.

14. Davies, *Jews in Eastern Poland and the USSR,* pp. 231–232.

15. Ibid., p. 234.

CHAPTER 6

1. From Chapter Seven, "Jews in Łódź After the War." Danuta Dabrowska and Abraham Wein, eds., *Encyclopedia of Jewish Communities, Poland: Łódź and Its Region.* Yad Vashem, 1976.

2. Ibid.

3. Chodakiewicz, Marek Jan, *After the Holocaust: Polish-Jewish Conflict in the Wake of World War II.* East European Monographs, 2003, p. 31.

4. Wolnerman, Ch., A. Burstin, and M.S. Geshuri, eds., *Oświęcim; Auschwitz Memorial Book.* Oshpitsin Society, 1977. Reference is in the section entitled, "Stones Tell the Tale."

5. Ibid.

6. "Finds No Reds in Ancient Krakow College Halls," *Chicago Daily Tribune,* Dec. 3, 1946.

7. "Polish Professors Deported to Reich," *The New York Times,* Nov. 25, 1939; and "The Past and the Present," essay on the Jagiellonian University Web site.

8. "Dr. Taubenschlag of Warsaw U., 77," *The New York Times,* June 27, 1958; and "Taubenschlag Was Suicide," *The New York Times,* June 28, 1958.

9. Lanzut Memorial Book, p. xxxiii.

10. "New Landed Poles Keep Old Ways on Farms Parceled from Estates," *The New York Times,* Jan. 12, 1945.

11. Lanzut Memorial Book, p. xix.

12. Schoenfeld, Joachim, *Holocaust Memoirs: Jews in the Lwów Ghetto, the Janowski Concentration Camp, and as Deportees in Siberia*. KTAV Publishing House, 1985, p. 153.

13. "Poles Declare Two Hoaxes Caused High Toll in Pogrom," *The New York Times*, July 6, 1946.

14. "Poland Executes 9 Pogrom Killers," *The New York Times*, July 16, 1946.

15. "100,000 More Jews Seen Fleeing Poland," *The New York Times*, Aug. 4, 1946; "Frantic Jews Rush to Cross Polish Border," *Chicago Daily Tribune*, July 7, 1946; and "Polish Jews' Exit Is Put at 20,000 since Pogrom." *The New York Times*, Aug. 15, 1946.

CHAPTER 7

1. Quoted in "Heidelberg," *Frank Leslie's Popular Monthly*, April 1887.

2. "Persecution of the Jews," *Times of London*, Feb. 4, 1936.

3. Much of this is from the university Website, www.uni-heidelberg.de. The description of the 550th-anniversary celebration is from "New Heidelberg," *Times of London*, June 29, 1936.

4. Quoted in "Aryan Science," *The Living Age*, Nov. 1938.

5. "Heidelberg Formally Reopens." *The New York Times*, Jan. 9, 1946; "Heidelberg Reopens," *The New York Times*, Jan. 13, 1946; and "U.S. Army Purges Heidelberg Staff," *The New York Times*, Mar. 28, 1946.

6. Quoted in "Heidelberg," *Frank Leslie's Popular Monthly*, April 1887.

7. Quoted in "Germany's Guilt-Complex: An Analysis and a Cure," *The New York Times*, Feb. 8, 1948.

8. Genizi, Haim, *America's Fair Share: The Admission and Resettlement of Displaced Persons, 1945–1952*. Wayne State University Press, 1993, p. 206.

9. The McCarran-Walter Act was eventually passed, over President Truman's veto, in June 1952. Luckily, we had arrived in New York City six months earlier.

CHAPTER 8

1. "Passover Marked Here and Abroad," *The New York Times*, Apr. 10, 1952.

2. "News of TV and Radio," *The New York Times*, Apr. 6, 1952.

3. Fabricant, Solomon, *Toward a Firmer Basis of Economic Policy: The Founding of the National Bureau of Economic Research*. NBER, 1984, p. 6.

4. Ibid.

5. Ibid.

6. Ibid., p. 3.

7. "U. of C. Pushes Plans for Business School," *Chicago Daily Tribune*, Nov. 28, 1958.

CHAPTER 9

1. "City Reservoirs Closed to Reds," *The New York Times*, May 7, 1957.
2. "Forecaster Not Apt to Climb Out on Limb," *Chicago Tribune*, June 21, 1965.
3. "The Oracles of Wall St.," *The New York Times*, Feb. 3, 1965.
4. "Indicators or Hunches," *Wall Street Journal*, June 6, 1967.
5. "Job Figures Reflect Shift to an Economy Based on Services," *The New York Times*, June 28, 1965; "Appraisal of Current Trends in Business and Finance," *Wall Street Journal*, June 28, 1965.
6. "The Crystal Ball Is Often Cloudy," *The New York Times*, July 3, 1966.

Index

About the Author

VICTOR ZARNOWITZ is one of the world's leading authorities on business cycles, business indicators, and forecast evaluation. He is Senior Fellow and Economic Counselor to the Conference Board. Dr. Zarnowitz is also Professor Emeritus of Economics and Finance, Graduate School of Business, The University of Chicago, and Research Associate, National Bureau of Economic Research. The recipient of many awards and honors, he is the author of *Business Cycles: Theory, History, Indicators, and Forecasting*.